MANAGING DIVERSITY IN
PUBLIC SECTOR WORKFORCES

Essentials of Public
Policy and Administration Series

Series Editor: Jay Shafritz
University of Pittsburgh

Westview Press proudly announces a new series of textbooks for public policy and administration courses. Written for students at both the advanced undergraduate level and graduate level, these texts follow a standard design and format which allows them to be incorporated easily into multiple courses. Each text covers a core aspect of public policy and administration that is commonly discussed in the classroom. They are written by authorities in their fields, and will serve as both core and supplemental texts.

New titles in the series include:

Managing Diversity in Public Sector Workforces
Norma M. Riccucci
Comparative Public Administration and Policy
Jamil E. Jreisat
The Regional Governing of Metropolitan America
David Miller

MANAGING DIVERSITY IN PUBLIC SECTOR WORKFORCES

Norma M. Riccucci

University at Albany, State University of New York

Westview
PRESS

A Member of the Perseus Books Group

Copyright © 2002 by Westview Press, A Member of the Perseus Books Group

Westview Press books are available at special discounts for bulk purchases in the United States by corporations, institutions, and other organizations. For more information, please contact the Special Markets Department at The Perseus Books Group, 11 Cambridge Center, Cambridge MA 02142, or call (617) 252-5298.

Published in 2002 in the United States of America by Westview Press, 5500 Central Avenue, Boulder, Colorado 80301–2877, and in the United Kingdom by Westview Press, 12 Hid's Copse Road, Cumnor Hill, Oxford OX2 9JJ

Find us on the World Wide Web at www.westviewpress.com

A CIP catalog record for this book is available from the Library of Congress.
ISBN 0-8133-3993-6 (HC)
ISBN 0-8133-9838-X (pbk.)
The paper used in this publication meets the requirements of the American National Standard for Permanence of Paper for Printed Library Materials Z39.48–1984.

10   9   8   7   6   5   4   3

For my loving brothers, John and Ricci

*Put your hand o'er your mouth when
you cough that'll help the solution.*

—STAPLE SINGERS,
"RESPECT YOURSELF"

CONTENTS

TABLES AND FIGURES

Tables

Figures

PREFACE

The topic of diversity or managing diversity has been at the top of public policy analysts' and public administrators' agendas for the past several years. It has been a matter of competitive survival, since the demographics of the workplace have dramatically changed over the last decade or so. The changes are having a significant effect on how organizations manage their workforces. The old styles of managing heterogeneous workforces are proving to be ineffectual, and so management strategies aimed at embracing diversity are essential. They can have positive implications for worker satisfaction and morale and, ultimately, the delivery of public services to the American people.

In addition, diversity in the broad sense may very well be a political bellwether for "affirmative action." Although this book focuses on managing diversity in the government workplace, the topics of affirmative action and equal employment opportunity (EEO) are also addressed because these policies, although different, are inextricably linked. Indeed, diversity has evolved from EEO and affirmative action, and yet it does not carry the negative connotations that at least affirmative action has carried for the last twenty years or so. The irony here is that diversity has always been the ultimate goal of affirmative action.

In sum, this book examines the demographic changes to the labor force and workforce and the ways in which government employers are managing or can prepare to manage diversity in their workplaces. It also addresses the implications of effectively managing diversity for the overall governance of American society.

ACKNOWLEDGMENTS

I would like to thank a number of people who read draft chapters, engaged in fruitful discussions, or helped generate ideas for this book. They include Jay M. Shafritz, University of Pittsburgh; Frank J. Thompson and Beryl A. Radin, both of Rockefeller College, University at Albany, SUNY; Carolyn Ban, University of Pittsburgh; David H. Rosenbloom, American University; Leo A. W. Wiegman, former executive editor, Westview Press; and Roxanne Wright, New York State's Governor's Office of Employee Relations.

I also extend my thanks to a number of persons who provided me with invaluable data sets for the research for this book. They include Randy E. Ilg of the U.S. Bureau of Labor Statistics; Paul van Rijn and John Palguta, both from the U.S. Merit Systems Protection Board; and Shonda L. Adams of the U.S. Office of Personnel Management.

—*Norma M. Riccucci*

1

Workforce Diversity and the Twenty-First Century

As we enter the third millennium, America's workforce looks markedly different than it ever has before. In a way, it can be described as poly-typic. Compared with the workforce of even twenty years ago, more white women, people of color, disabled persons, new and recent immigrants, gays and lesbians, and intergenerational mixes (i.e., baby boomers, Generation Xers, and Generation Nexters) now work in America. To say that this has created challenges for managing the workplace is an understatement. The way in which government employers embrace this opportunity of diversity will clearly distinguish effective and efficient organizations from those that are unproductive and unable to meet the demands and necessities of the American people in the twenty-first century.

Today, public and private sector employers are poised to create productive workforces that are truly representative of not simply the national but the *global* population. This book will examine the demographic changes to the labor force and workplace and the ways in which government employers are managing the imminently diverse populations that now fill public sector jobs. It will address the specific management strategies and initiatives relied on by public sector employers as well as the implications of effectively managing variegated workforces for the overall governance of American society. Although the book does not address the normative considerations around the importance of diversity, it certainly makes clear the reality that demographic changes to the population in general have, as a corollary, led to changes in the labor pools from which both public and private sector employers draw their workers. In short, workforce diver-

TABLE 1.1   Comparing EEO, Affirmative Action, and Managing Diversity

EEO	Affirmative Action	Managing Diversity
Qualitative/Quantitative. Emphasis is on preventing or ending discrimination	*Qualitative/Quantitative.* Emphasis is on redressing past discrimination and achieving diverse, representative workforces	*Behavioral.* Emphasis is on building specific skills and creating a productive work environment with the organization's human resources
Legally driven. Mandated by federal law	*Managerially and legally driven.* Involves voluntarily developed goals as well as court-ordered programs. Common law has defined its legality and constitutionality	*Strategically driven.* Behaviors and policies are seen as contributing to organizational goals and objectives such as productivity
Fairness. Seeks to end discrimination and create equal opportunities	*Remedial and compensatory.* Specific voluntarily developed goals as well as court-ordered programs.	*Pragmatic.* The organization benefits in terms of morale and increases in productivity
Access Model. Model assumes that protected-class persons will be able to access organizations	*Assimilation model.* Model assumes that persons and groups brought into the system will adapt to existing organizational norms. Can result in "sink or swim" atmosphere/environment	*Synergy model.* Model seeks to change organizational culture to accommodate diverse groups. Assumes people will develop new ways of working together in a pluralistic environment
Level playing field. Seeks to ensure equal opportunity and access	*Opens doors.* Seeks to affect hiring and promotion decisions in organizations	*Opens the system.* Seeks to affect managerial practices and policies

Sources: Adapted from Riccucci (1997), Henderson (1994), and Gardenswartz and Rowe (1993).

sity will prevail in public and private sector organizations in the twenty-first century. To the extent that the demographics of the workforce reflect that of the general population that it serves *and* it is effectively managed, the delivery of public services will be greatly enhanced.[1]

Diversity qua Diversity

When we speak of managing diversity in the context of the workplace, we often think of concepts such as equal employment opportunity (EEO) and affirmative action. Although diversity has evolved from these concepts, it is significantly different. The easiest way to understand the differences in these concepts is to compare and contrast them. Table 1.1 illustrates the conceptual differences and similarities between and among EEO, affirmative action, and managing diversity.

As the table shows, EEO is largely viewed as a means to prevent discrimination in the workplace on the basis of such factors or characteristics as race, color, religion, gender, national origin, ability, and age. Affirmative action, on the other hand, which emerged in response to pervasive employment discrimination, embodies proactive efforts to redress past discriminations as well as to diversify the workplace in terms of race, ethnicity, gender, physical abilities, and so forth. Affirmative action has been viewed as a legal tool to ensure equal employment opportunity or diversity. Its emphasis on proaction has been the cause of endless controversy and public debate over its use as an employment tool or social policy. Indeed, opponents to affirmative action very early on were quick to label it "reverse discrimination."

Managing diversity is the next iteration on the continuum. It refers to the ability of top management to develop strategies as well as programs and policies to manage and accommodate diversity in their workplaces. It includes the ability of organizations to harness the diverse human resources available in order to create a productive and motivated workforce. Key here is management's ability to develop ways to address such challenges as communication breakdowns, misunderstandings, and even hostilities that invariably result from working in an environment with persons from highly diverse backgrounds, age cohorts, and lifestyles.[2] Also key is that diversity becomes a goal of the organization and is *integrated into the overall strategic goals* of the organization.

The opportunities are abundant, and the efficacy with which they are seized by public employers will determine the ability of governments to successfully serve the needs and interests of the American populace.

The Demographics of the Labor Force and Workplace

Predictions and estimates over the past twenty years or so suggest that because of demographic changes to this nation's population, the composition of public and private sector workplaces is contemporaneously changing. The workforce changes that have already begun to occur include:

1. Increases in the number of women
2. Increases in the number of people of color
3. Increases in the average age of workers
4. Increases in the number of foreign-born or immigrant workers
5. Increases in the number of contingent workers (e.g., part-timers, temporary workers)

A very simple yet striking way to portray the demographic shifts, at least as they pertain to white men, women, and people of color, is presented in Figure 1.1. As the data show, women will account for about 48

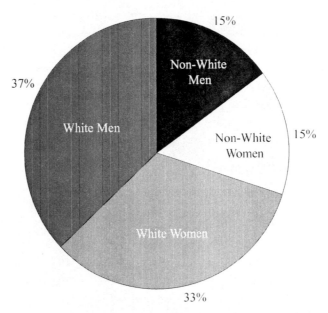

Source: Based on data obtained from the Bureau of Labor Statistics (BLS) Web site:
http://stats.bls.gov.

FIGURE 1.1   The Complexion of the U.S. Workforce by 2008

percent of the workforce by the year 2008. White men will account for about 37 percent and men of color around 15 percent.

Table 1.2 provides greater detail on important demographic changes that have implications for employment. It illustrates changes in the workforce based on gender, race, and ethnicity from 1978 to 1998 and projected changes to 2008. The table shows a decline in the participation of white men in the workforce, with an increase of white women (12.1 percent). In addition, the table shows remarkable increases of women of color in the workforce, while the projections for men of color show slight decreases in their workforce participation.

Figure 1.2 shows a clearer picture of the changes in workforce participation of women from 1978 to 2008.

Table 1.3 illustrates the aging of the labor force. As we can see, there is a steady increase in the forty and older age-group. By 2008, this age cohort is expected to represent a majority share of the civilian labor force for both women and men. Although there are drops in labor force partic-

TABLE 1.2 Workforce Participation Rates, 16 Years and Older, by Gender, Race, and Ethnicity, 1978, 1988, 1998, and Projected 2008

Group	Percentage Rate (percentage)					Percentage Point Change (percentage)
	1978	1988	1996	1998	2008	1978 – 2008
White	63.3	66.2	67.2	67.3	67.9	4.6
Men	78.6	76.9	75.8	75.6	74.5	-4.1
Women	49.4	56.4	59.1	59.4	61.5	12.1
African American	61.5	63.8	64.1	65.6	66.3	4.8
Men	71.7	71.0	68.7	69.0	68.3	-3.4
Women	53.2	58.0	60.4	62.8	64.6	11.4
Asian and other [a]	64.6	65.0	65.8	67.0	66.9	2.3
Men	75.9	74.4	73.4	75.5	74.0	-1.9·
Women	54.1	56.5	58.8	59.2	60.5	6.4
Hispanic origin [b]	-	67.4	66.5	67.9	67.7	0.3
Men	-	81.9	79.6	79.8	77.9	-0.4
Women	-	53.2	53.4	55.6	57.9	4.7

Source: Bureau of Labor Statistics (BLS) Web site: http://stats.bls.gov. (Participation refers to the percentage of a specific group participating in the workforce. So, by 2008, for example, 61.5 percent of all women will be participating in the workforce.)

Notes:

[a] The "Asian and other" group includes (1) Asians and Pacific Islanders and (2) American Indians and Alaska Natives. The historical data are derived by subtracting "black" from the "black and other" group; projections are made directly, not by subtraction.

[b] Data by Hispanic origin are not available before 1980. Percentage point change is calculated from 1988 to 2008.

ipation of the younger age cohorts, the changing *values* of younger generations (e.g., the Generation Xers and Nexters) will create challenges for government managers to the extent that younger and aging persons will be working alongside one another.

Changes to the labor force and workforce go well beyond race, ethnicity, gender, and age. As noted, there will be greater diversity based on such characteristics or factors as ability, sexual orientation, foreign-born status, and so forth. For example, greater protections offered to disabled persons under the Americans with Disabilities Act (ADA) of 1990 has increased their representation in public and private sector workforces. And the ADA has relatively strong provisions requiring employers to make "reasonable accommodations" for disabled persons.

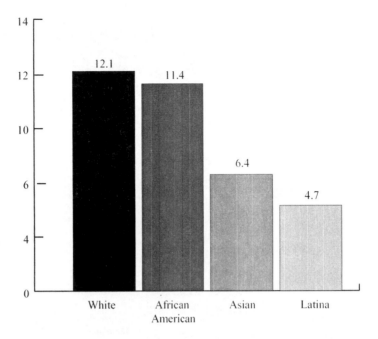

FIGURE 1.2   Percentage Change in Women's Workforce Participation, 1978 to Projected 2008

This includes making modifications or adjustments to a job or the work environment in order to enable the worker with a disability to perform the job.

Likewise, there are increasing numbers of gays and lesbians in the workplace, perhaps due to state and local laws and regulations that prohibit discrimination based on sexual orientation.[3] (There is no federal law that prohibits discrimination against gays and lesbians in the workplace.) Data on the percentages of gays and lesbians in public sector workforces are extremely difficult to collect. Employers are not allowed to inquire about sexual orientation, nor are employees required to disclose their sexual orientation. Notwithstanding, the number of gays and lesbians "coming out" in the workplace is growing, and we are seeing more and more employers offering domestic partnership benefits that serve the needs and interests of not only the partners of gays and lesbians but the partners of heterosexual workers as well.

TABLE 1.3   Distribution of the Labor Force by Age and Gender, 1978, 1988, 1998, and Projected 2008 (Percentage)

| | Labor Force | | | |
Group	1978	1988	1998	2008
Total, 16 years and older	100.0	100.0	100.0	100.0
16 to 24	24.5	18.5	15.9	16.3
25 to 39	36.0	42.3	37.6	31.9
40 and older	39.6	39.2	46.5	51.7
65 and older	3.0	2.7	2.8	3.0
75 and older	0.4	0.4	0.5	0.5
Men, 16 years and older	100.0	100.0	100.0	100.0
16 to 24	22.6	17.6	15.5	16.1
25 to 39	36.6	42.6	38.0	32.2
40 and older	40.8	39.9	46.5	51.8
65 and older	3.2	2.9	3.0	3.4
75 and older	0.5	0.5	0.6	0.6
Women, 16 years and older	100.0	100.0	100.0	100.0
16 to 24	27.1	19.7	16.4	16.6
25 to 39	35.1	41.9	37.1	31.7
40 and older	37.8	38.4	46.6	51.7
65 and older	2.7	2.4	2.5	2.5
75 and older	0.3	0.3	0.4	0.4

Source: Bureau of Labor Statistics (BLS) Web site: http://stats.bls.gov.

The contingent workforce (e.g., part-timers, temporary workers, and retirees returning to work) has also been growing steadily since the 1980s due to a variety of factors, such as the changing needs and interests of workers. From 1980 to 1988, the number of part-time workers increased to 21 percent of the workforce, and for the same time period, the number of temporary workers increased by a staggering 175 percent.[4] The contingent workforce is also part of the "new workplace" and will require attention from government employers, particularly since these workers are sometimes found to be less dedicated and motivated, with lower levels of overall performance or productivity.

The U.S. Census Bureau reports a steady increase in the population of immigrants to the United States. Between 1970 and 1980, almost 4.5 million immigrants legally entered the United States, and in the 1980s, legal immigrants accounted for 30 percent of the nation's population growth.[5] Labor statistics indicate that legal immigrants composed 7 percent of America's workforce in the mid-1980s and has increased to over 20 percent as we move into the twenty-first century. Most of the immigrants have settled in the South and the West, and they represent a broad spectrum in terms of socioeconomic status. It seems clear, based on past and current trends, that the United States will continue to be a strong magnet for Latin American, Asian, and Eastern European populations.

Finally, it should be noted that rapid technological change in our society creates challenges for how work is done and the skills required to do it. Innovations in computing, telecommunications, and information technology have implications for all workers in the public and private sectors. The challenge for government employers is to ensure that *all* of their workers possess the tools and skills to perform the new jobs.

In sum, the nature of public and private sector workforces has undergone considerable change in the last several decades, and it will continue on this trajectory into the twenty-first century. Public sector employers are challenged to seize the opportunities presented by the new workplace in order to better serve the American people.

Scope of the Book

This book addresses diversity in public employment. To be sure, references must inevitably be made to the private sector and educational settings, especially in the context of EEO and affirmative action. Notwithstanding, public employment serves as the main arena for this book.

Because diversity has evolved from EEO and affirmative action, Chapter 2 will provide a cursory account of these topics and will illustrate the extent to which EEO and affirmative action are still relied on in the workplace. Chapters 3–7 address the core of managing diversity in the public sector. These chapters examine the initiatives, strategies, and programs that government employers either do or might rely on to ensure that the demographic mosaic embodied by their workforces is prepared to meet the needs and interests of the American citizenry of the twenty-first century. Separate chapters address each of the following aspects of diversity: race and ethnicity (including immigrants), gender, physical ability, age, and sexual orientation. It is important to note that in light of the subject matter, the research approach for this book is necessarily based in both description and prescription.

Notes

1. The topic of "representative bureaucracy" looks at the degree to which government bureaucracies are demographically representative of the general populations they serve. It is not the focus of this book, however, which operates from the premise that diversity does indeed exist but needs to be managed effectively in order for government workforces to be efficient and productive in the delivery of public services.

2. Norma Carr-Ruffino, *Diversity Success Strategies* (Boston: Butterworth Heinemann, 1999).

3. Charles W. Gossett, "Lesbians and Gay Men in the Public Sector Work Force," in Carolyn Ban and Norma M. Riccucci, eds., *Public Personnel Management: Current Concerns, Future Challenges*, 2d ed. (New York: Longman, 1997), pp. 123–138.

4. Mak Khojasteh, "Workforce 2000: Demographic Changes and Their Impacts," *International Journal of Public Administration* 17, no. 3 4 (1994): 465 505.

5. Khojasteh, "Workforce 2000."

Additional Reading

Best Practices in Achieving Workforce Diversity. Washington, D.C.: U.S. Department of Commerce and the National Partnership for Reinventing Government Benchmarking Study, 2000.

Fullerton, Howard N., Jr. "Labor Force Projections to 2008: Steady Growth and Changing Composition." *Monthly Labor Review*, November 1999, pp. 19–32.

Gardenswartz, Lee, and Anita Rowe. *Managing Diversity: A Complete Desk Reference and Planning Guide*. Homewood, Ill.: Business One Irwin, 1993.

Golembiewski, Robert T. *Managing Diversity in Organizations*. Tuscaloosa: University of Alabama Press, 1995.

Henderson, George. *Cultural Diversity in the Workplace*. Westport, Conn.: Quorum, 1994.

Kellough, J. Edward and Katherine C. Naff, "Managing Diversity in the Federal Service." Paper presented at the Sixth National Public Management Research Conference, 2001, Bloomington, Indiana.

Klingner, Donald E. "Work Force Diversity." In Jay M. Shafritz, ed., *International Encyclopedia for Public Policy and Administration*. New York: Henry Holt, 1998.

Loden, Marilyn, and Judy B. Rosener. *Workforce America!* Homewood, Ill.: Business One Irwin, 1991.

Naff, Katharine C. *To Look Like America: Dismantling Barriers for Women and Minorities in Government*. Boulder: Westview, 2001.

Ospina, Sonia M. *Illusions of Opportunity: Employee Expectations and Workplace Inequality*. Ithaca, N.Y.: Cornell University Press, 1996.

Riccucci, Norma M. "Will Affirmative Action Survive into the Twenty-First Century?" In Carolyn Ban and Norma M. Riccucci, eds., *Public Personnel Management: Current Concerns, Future Challenges*, pp. 57–72. 2d ed. New York: Longman, 1997.

U.S. Office of Personnel Management. *Building and Maintaining a Diverse, High-Quality Workforce.* Washington, D.C., 2000.

Wise, Lois Recascino, and Mary Tschirhart. "Examining Empirical Evidence on Diversity Effects: How Useful Is Diversity Research for Public-Sector Managers." *Public Administration Review,* September-October 2000, pp. 386–394.

Wise, Lois Recascino, Mary Tschirhart, Deborah K. Hosinski, and Lana Bandy. *Diversity Research: A Meta-Analysis.* Stockholm, Sweden: Institute for Future Studies, 1997.

Wooldridge, Blue; Barbara Clark Maddox; and Yan Zhang. "Changing Demographics of the Work Force: Implications for the Design of Productive Work Environments: An Exploratory Analysis." *Review of Public Personnel Administration,* 15, 1995, pp. 60–72.

Wooldridge, Blue and Jennifer Wester. "The Turbulent Environment of Public Personnel Administration: Responding to the Challenge of Changing Workplace of the Twenty-First Century." *Public Personnel Management,* 40, 1991, pp. 207–224.

Workforce 2020. Indianapolis: Hudson Institute, 1997.

2

Affirmative Action and Equal Employment Opportunity

In a very fundamental sense, issues surrounding diversity in the workplace are inextricably linked to equal employment opportunity (EEO) and affirmative action. As noted in Chapter 1, EEO seeks to end discrimination in the workplace, and affirmative action is a means to producing a diverse workforce. Any attempt to understand measures aimed at promoting, maintaining, and managing diversity—the next iteration of EEO and affirmative action—should logically begin with a brief review of EEO and affirmative action.

The Evolution of EEO and Affirmative Action

Equal employment opportunity (EEO) refers to policies aimed at preventing employment discrimination. In this sense, EEO policies and laws were developed in response to discriminatory practices against persons based on race, color, gender, religion, national origin, disability, age, and so forth. Table 2.1 provides a snapshot of the EEO laws and policies that have been advanced since the Reconstruction era. It is worth pointing out that despite the ratification of the Fourteenth Amendment to the U.S. Constitution in 1868 and enactment of the Civil Rights Acts of 1866 and 1871, which would eventually be relied on to enforce the Fourteenth Amendment, serious attention to preventing discrimination in the workplace did not begin until one hundred years later.

In the 1960s the United States, spurred by racial unrest, was galvanized into taking genuine action to end discriminatory employment practices. In 1964, Title VII of the Civil Rights Act, the cornerstone of EEO law, was

TABLE 2.1 Federal EEO Law

Law/Policy	Provisions/Coverage
Civil Rights Act of 1866, Section 1981	Provides that "all persons shall have the Same right . . . to the full and equal benefit of the laws . . . as is enjoyed by white citizens."
Fourteenth Amendment to U.S. Constitution (1868)	Requires all states and their political subdivisions to provide equal protection of the laws to all persons in their jurisdictions.
Civil Rights Act of 1871, Section 198	Prohibits persons acting "under color of any statute, ordinance, regulation, custom or usage..." from depriving any citizen or person within the jurisdiction of the U.S. of any rights, privileges, or immunities secured by the Constitution.
Ramspect Act 1940	Prohibits discrimination in federal employment based on race, color, or creed.
Executive Order 8802 (1941)	Called for the elimination of discrimination based on race, color, religion, or national origin with the federal service and defense production industries.
Civil Rights Act of 1964, Title VII	Prohibits discrimination on the basis of race, color, religion, gender, and national origin.
Executive Order 11246, as amended (1965)	Forbids employment discrimination based on race, color, religion, gender, and national origin by federal government and federal contractors and subcontractors, and requires the federal government and contractors to engage in affirmative action to hire and promote persons based on these characteristics.
Age Discrimination in Employment Act (ADEA), as amended (1967)	Forbids employment discrimination based on age.
Equal Employment Opportunity Act of 1972 (amends Title VII of CRA of 1964)	Extends Title VII protection to state, local, federal government employees and workers in educational institutions.
Vocational Rehabilitation Act of 1973	Prohibits federal government and its contractors from discriminating against persons with disabilities.

TABLE 2.1   Federal EEO Law (*continued*)

Law/Policy	Provisions/Coverage
Vietnam Era Veterans' Readjustment Act of 1974	Requires the federal government and its contractors to promote employment opportunities for Vietnam-era veterans.
Americans with Disabilities Act (1990)	Forbids private, state, and local government employers from discriminating on the basis of disability.
Civil Rights Act of 1991	Overturned several negative U.S. Supreme Court decisions issued in 1989 on EEO and affirmative action; established a Glass Ceiling Commission to study artificial barriers to the advancement of women and persons of color in the workplace.

passed. Title VII is intended to prevent private sector employers with fifteen or more employees from discriminating on the basis of race, color, religion, gender, and national origin. Parenthetically, civil rights efforts at the time revolved mainly around issues of race. Thus EEO measures were largely aimed at ending employment discrimination against African Americans. Adding "sex" to Title VII as a proscribed category of discrimination was a conscious effort to gut the entire Civil Rights Act. Congressperson Howard "Judge" Smith of Virginia was a leading opponent of civil rights for African Americans. It was his unauthorized absence from Congress in 1957, putatively to inspect a burning barn on his property in Virginia, that prevented Congress from acting on a bill that year to prevent employment discrimination. To Smith, the only thing more ludicrous than equal rights for African Americans was equal rights for women.[1] By adding gender discrimination to the Title VII language, he was confident that the civil rights bill would be defeated. His efforts, however, backfired—because the momentum for a civil rights act was so immense at the time, the 1964 act passed, now with protections for women in the workforce as well.

As Table 2.1 shows, Title VII of the Civil Rights Act was extended to public employers with passage of the Equal Employment Opportunity Act in 1972. It is this act, along with provisions of the U.S. Constitution (e.g., the Fourteenth Amendment) and its enforcing legislation (Sections 1981 and 1983 of the Civil Rights Acts of 1866 and 1871, respectively), that serve as the primary legal mechanisms to protect women and people of color from employment discrimination in the public sector.[2]

As with race, ethnicity, and gender, employers are prohibited from discriminating against persons on a number of other dimensions or characteristics, including age, ability, and even veterans status. For example, the Age Discrimination in Employment Act (ADEA) of 1967, as amended, makes it illegal for private businesses to refuse to hire, discharge, or otherwise discriminate against an individual between the ages of forty and seventy. The act was amended in 1974 to apply to state and local governments. Age discrimination in federal employment is prohibited by executive order, but additional amendments to the ADEA banned forced retirement for federal employees at any age. Enforcement authority over the ADEA was originally vested in the Department of Labor but was transferred to the EEOC as part of the federal civil service reform of 1978.

There are also various laws that prohibit discrimination on the basis of a disability. For instance, the Vocational Rehabilitation Act of 1973 as amended prohibits discrimination against disabled persons. These protections were strengthened by Title I of the Americans with Disabilities Act (ADA) of 1990, which covers private sector employers as well as state and local government employers with fifteen or more employees. The federal workforce, which is not protected by the ADA, continues to be covered by the Rehabilitation Act of 1973. An important aspect of the ADA is that it covers persons who are HIV positive or have AIDS.

From EEO to Affirmative Action

Equal employment opportunity law is considered passive in the sense that it requires employers to refrain from discriminating against protected-class members (i.e., those designated for protection by the specific EEO legislation). Affirmative action, however, requires employers to take positive steps toward employing, promoting, and retaining qualified women, people of color, and other protected-class persons (see description of Executive Order 11246, as amended, in Table 2.1). Not only would this help rectify past and present discrimination, but it would also help create "representative bureaucracies," that is, government bureaucracies that are demographically representative of the general populations that they serve. Because affirmative action is based on proactive efforts, it has led to myriad lawsuits challenging its legality and constitutionality.[3] Although a lengthy discussion of the entire set of case law goes beyond the scope of this book, Table 2.2 provides a chronological summary of the legal actions around affirmative action from the point of "ground zero": the U.S. Supreme Court's landmark *Regents of the University of California v. Bakke* ruling in 1978.

TABLE 2.2   The Chronology of Legal Actions Around Affirmative Action

1978	*Regents of the University of California v. Bakke.* U.S. Supreme Court upholds the principle of affirmative action, but strikes down its operation by the University at California under the Fourteenth Amendment and Title VI of the Civil Rights Act of 1964.
1979	*United Steelworkers of America v. Weber.* U.S. Supreme Court upholds legality of voluntarily developed affirmative action plan under Title VII of Civil Rights Act of 1964.
1980	*Fullilove v. Klutznick.* U.S. Supreme Court upholds constitutionality (under Fifth and Fourteenth Amendments) of federal set-aside programs enacted by the U.S. Congress.
1984	*Firefighters Local Union and Memphis Fire Department v. Stotts.* U.S. Supreme Court upholds, under Title VII of the Civil Rights Act, as amended, the use of a seniority system in layoff decisions, despite its negative impact on affirmative action.
1986	*Wygant v. Jackson Bd. of Ed.* U.S. Supreme Court strikes down, under the Fourteenth Amendment to the U.S. Constitution, the use of affirmative action in layoff decisions.
1986	*Sheet Metal Workers' International Association v. EEOC.* U.S. Supreme Court upholds, under Title VII and Fifth Amendment to the U.S. Constitution, a court-ordered affirmative action program to remedy past discrimination by a union and apprenticeship committee against people of color.
1986	*Int'l Assoc. of Firefighters v. City of Cleveland.* U.S. Supreme Court upholds, under Title VII, affirmative action consent decree that provided for the use of race-conscious relief in promotion decisions.
1987	*Johnson v. Transportation Agency, Santa Clara County.* U.S. Supreme Court upholds, under Title VII, voluntarily developed affirmative action program intended to correct gender and racial imbalances in traditionally segregated job categories.
1987	*U.S. v. Paradise.* U.S. Supreme Court upholds, under the Fourteenth Amendment to the U.S. Constitution, a court-ordered affirmative action plan aimed at remedying discrimination against African Americans in hiring and promotion decisions in Alabama Public Safety Department.
1989	*City of Richmond v Croson.* U.S. Supreme Court strikes down the constitutionality, under the Fourteenth Amendment, of a local government's set-aside program because it could not satisfy the criteria of the strict scrutiny test.

TABLE 2.2 The Chronology of Legal Actions Around Affirmative Action (*continued*)

1989	*Martin v. Wilks.* U.S. Supreme Court allowed white firefighters to challenge, under Title VII, an affirmative action consent decree to which they were not a party, years after it had been approved by a lower court.
1990	*Metro Broadcasting v. F.C.C.* U.S. Supreme Court upholds the constitutionality (under Fifth Amendment) of F.C.C.'s set-aside policy, which bears the imprimatur of longstanding congressional support.
1990	Civil Rights Acts vetoed by President Bush. Congress fails to override veto.
1991	Civil Rights Act passed. Restores affirmative action to its pre-1989 legal status.
1995	*Adarand v. Peña.* U.S. Supreme Court rules that the Equal Protection Clause of the Fifth Amendment requires that racial classifications used in federal set-aside programs must undergo strict scrutiny analysis.
1995	*In re Birmingham Reverse Discrimination Employment Litigation (BRDEL).* U.S. Supreme Court let stand, without comment, a decision by the U.S. Court of Appeals for the Eleventh Circuit that invalidated a promotion plan aimed at promoting African American firefighters to the position of lieutenant.
1995	*Claus v. Duquesne Light Company.* U.S. Supreme Court let stand, without comment, a decision by the Third Circuit Court of Appeals, which awarded a white engineer for a utility company $425,000 in damages because, according to the court, he was "passed over" in favor of an African American for promotion to a managerial job.
1996	*Hopwood v. State of Texas.* U.S. Supreme Court let stand a ruling by the U.S. Court of Appeals for the Fifth Circuit, that struck down the constitutionality of an affirmative action program at the University of Texas Law School.
1996	President Clinton suspends, for a minimum of three years, all federal set-aside programs.
1997	*Taxman v. Piscataway Township Board of Education* is dropped from the U.S. Supreme Court's calendar because parties settled. Thus remains the 1996 opinion of U.S. Court of Appeals for the Third Circuit: the goal of achieving or maintaining diversity cannot be a justification under Title VII of the Civil Rights Act as amended for a race-based employment decision.

TABLE 2.2 The Chronology of Legal Actions Around Affirmative Action (*continued*)

1999	*Lesage v. Texas.* U.S. Supreme Court throws out a reverse discrimination suit filed under the Equal Protection Clause of the Fourteenth Amendment against the University of Texas' Department of Education.
2000	*Smith v. University of Washington.* Relying on the Bakke ruling, the Ninth Circuit Court of Appeals upholds a race-based affirmative action program for admissions stating that a properly designed and operated race-conscious admissions program would not be in violation of Title VI or the Fourteenth Amendment.

Note: Actions around EEO or employment discrimination law (e.g., the U.S. Supreme Court's 1971 ruling in *Griggs v. Duke Power Co.,* 401 U.S. 424) are not addressed here.

Perhaps the most important legal developments around affirmative action as of this writing include the following cases: *Hopwood, Piscataway, Smith,* and *Lesage*.[4] A brief discussion of these cases is in order because they represent key augmentations around the current status of affirmative action. For example, as indicated in Table 2.2, the U.S. Supreme Court let stand the U.S. Court of Appeals for the Fifth Circuit's decision in *Hopwood v. State of Texas* (5th Cir. 1996). The Fifth Circuit Court in *Hopwood* struck down the constitutionality of an affirmative action program at the University of Texas law school aimed at increasing the number of African American and Mexican American students. In reversing the district court's decision, the appeals court issued a ruling that did not necessarily evaluate the actual admissions program of the law school, but rather ruled more broadly on the constitutionality of using race as a criterion in admissions decisions.[5] In effect, the ruling called into question the continued validity of the High Court's 1978 *Bakke* ruling.

For now, the *Hopwood* ruling governs at least the three states encompassed by the Fifth Circuit—Texas, Louisiana, and Mississippi—because the U.S. Supreme Court, in July 1996, said it would not hear the appeal by the state of Texas from the Fifth Circuit's ruling.

In the *Taxman v. Piscataway Township Board of Education* case, this New Jersey school board, faced with budget problems, was forced to lay off teachers. In an effort to maintain racial diversity in its teaching staff, the school board dismissed Sharon Taxman, a white teacher, rather than the equally qualified African American teacher, Debra Williams, the only person of color in the Business Department out of ten other teachers. Both had accrued an equal amount of seniority because they were hired the same day. In this case, the U.S. Court of Appeals for the Third Circuit ruled that the goal of achieving or maintaining diversity cannot be a justification for a race-based employment decision under Title VII of the Civil Rights Act as amended. It went on to say that affirmative action could only be justified as a remedy for past discrimination. The U.S. Supreme Court agreed to hear an appeal to the case,[6] but before the case went before the High Court, the parties settled. Taxman received $186,000 in the settlement, with her lawyers receiving $247,500. Thus the Third Circuit's opinion stands.

In contrast with the *Hopwood* and *Piscataway* decisions is the Ninth Circuit Appellate Court ruling in *Smith v. University of Washington* (2000), where the appeals court upheld an admissions policy at the University of Washington law school that effectively takes race into account. In *Smith*, three white applicants to the law school sued for the school's use of affirmative action in admissions decisions. The applicants claimed that they were denied admissions to the law school because racial preferences were granted to people of color. Race was considered as one of several diversity factors in making admissions decisions at least until November 1998, when Washington's voter initiative Measure 200 was passed. Similar to Proposition 209 in California, Washington's I-200 bans the use of affirmative action in state and local hiring, contracting, and education.

Subsequent to passage of I-200, the university's law school developed a new admissions policy that retained a "diversity clause." The policy stated that "important academic objectives are furthered by . . . students . . . from diverse backgrounds" and then went on to set out a list of factors that would promote diversity, including

> persevering or personal adversity or other social hardships; having lived in a foreign country or spoken a language other than English at home; career goals; employment history; educational background; . . . geographic diversity or unique life experiences. (*Smith v. University of Washington* 2000, 1192)

Because the terms "race," "color," and "national origin" were not included in the list, the appeals court upheld the policy. The Ninth Circuit court stated that

> [t]he district court correctly decided that Justice Powell's opinion in *Bakke* described the law and would require a determination that a properly

designed and operated race-conscious admissions program at the law school
of the University of Washington would not be in violation of Title VI or the
Fourteenth Amendment. It was also correct when it determined that *Bakke*
has not been overruled by the Supreme Court. Thus, at our level of the judicial system Justice Powell's opinion remains the law. (*Smith v. University of
Washington* 2000, 1201)

One of the most recent cases as of this writing is *Lesage v. Texas*. In this
case, Lesage, an African immigrant of Caucasian descent, applied for
admission to a Ph.D. program in the Education Department of the
University of Texas at Austin. Of the 233 applications received, about
twenty students were admitted to the program. Lesage was not admitted,
but one person of color out of the twenty was offered admission. Lesage
discovered that race was a factor at some stage in the admissions review
process and filed a "reverse discrimination" suit, claiming that his rights
under the Equal Protection Clause of the Fourteenth Amendment had
been violated.

The district court in *Lesage* ruled that there was "no evidence that race
was a factor in the decision to deny [Lesage's] admission to the . . . program" and that there was "uncontested evidence that the students ultimately admitted to the program had credentials that the committee considered superior to" Lesage's (*Lesage v. Texas*, 1997 at 7). The district court
thus ruled against Lesage and in favor of the university.

On appeal, the Fifth Circuit Appellate Court reversed the lower court's
decision. However, the court did not review the district court's conclu-
sion regarding whether Lesage would have otherwise been admitted to
the program (i.e., if there was no affirmative action, or race-based consideration). The appeals court instead ruled that the university violated
Lesage's constitutional rights by "rejecting his application in the course
of operating a racially discriminatory admissions program (*Lesage v.
Texas*, 158 F.3d at 222). It was the Fifth Circuit that struck down the affirmative action program at the University of Texas in *Hopwood*; its decision
in *Lesage*, then, was somewhat anticipated.

The U.S. Supreme Court, however, in a surprising decision, reversed
the judgment of the appeals court. Although the Court did not decide
whether the university's admissions process was discriminatory, it ruled
that the court of appeals erred in its judgment that it was "irrelevant" as
to whether Lesage would have been admitted to the university in the
absence of an affirmative action program. The Supreme Court stated that
the Appeals Court of the Fifth Circuit failed to adhere to the High Court's

well-established framework for analyzing claims similar to the ones arising in *Lesage*. Referring to earlier decisions, the Court said that "even if
the government has considered an impermissible criterion in making a
decision adverse to the plaintiff, it can nonetheless defeat liability by
demonstrating that it would have made the same decision absent the for-
bidden consideration." This wording suggests that public employers and
universities can avoid liability in constitutional challenges to their affirmative action programs by demonstrating that they would have made
the same decision (e.g., to hire or admit a person of color) without the
affirmative action program. The *Lesage* decision also leads to questions as
to how the Supreme Court might have ruled on *Hopwood*, had it agreed
to review the case.

In sum, the contours of affirmative action law continue to be reshaped
by the courts. Although affirmative action programs have been hard-
pressed to meet certain constitutional challenges or standards (e.g., the
strict scrutiny test), employers can certainly mount defenses along the
lines of demonstrating that they would have made the same decision to
hire a protected-class person even in the absence of an affirmative action
program. This is a well-established approach in cases involving the liability and immunity of public officials and organizations facing constitutional challenges.[7] Indeed, this is the implication of the Supreme Court's
opinion in *Lesage*, as discussed above. It is also worth noting that the
courts continue to be willing to uphold the legality of affirmative action
programs under Title VII if used as a remedy for past discrimination, as
the Third Circuit Court of Appeals made clear in its *Piscataway* decision.
And some courts, as the *Smith* decision suggests, will go even further in
upholding race-based affirmative action programs.

From EEO and Affirmative Action to Diversity

One of the most important points to be made from this cursory review of
EEO and affirmative action law is that, despite the legal rulings around
affirmative action, public and private sector employers continue to rely
on affirmative action as well as other tools and techniques to rectify
employment discrimination or to *diversify* their workforces. Moreover,
affirmative action continues to be an important tool for the promotion of
protected-class persons to upper-level positions in the workplace.
Indeed, as will be seen later in this book, diversity measures must go
beyond entry-level hiring. Managing diversity involves ensuring that
every reach of the organizational hierarchy is diversified and that the

workplace is free from the hostilities and harassment that often arise in a highly diverse workforce.

California provides a good example of government employers' continued use of affirmative action, despite court as well as *voter* action. In 1996, the voter initiative Proposition 209 was passed; it forbids the use of affirmative action in public employment, public education, and public contracting in the state of California. The constitutionality of Proposition 209 was challenged shortly afterward in *Coalition for Economic Equity v. Pete Wilson* (1996). In this case, a federal district court judge ruled that Proposition 209 was unconstitutional, opining that the controversial measure violated the equal protection guarantees of California's women and people of color. The judge effectively blocked the enforcement of Proposition 209 by issuing a preliminary injunction, concluding that the law discriminated against women and people of color by banning "constitutionally permissible" affirmative action programs.

A year later, the U.S. Court of Appeals for the Ninth Circuit, whose jurisdiction includes California, reversed the district court's decision and ordered the district court judge to lift the temporary injunction (see *Coalition for Economic Equity v. Pete Wilson*, 1997). The appellate court's ruling, in effect, upheld Proposition 209. The Ninth Circuit ruled that Proposition 209 was constitutional and that it did not violate the equal protection guarantees of women and people of color. Parenthetically, the panel of circuit court judges in *Coalition for Economic Equity* differed from the panel that presided over the *Smith v. University of Washington* decision, discussed earlier. It may be recalled that in *Smith*, the Ninth Circuit panel upheld an affirmative action program in university admissions that takes race into account.

In November 1997, the U.S. Supreme Court rejected a challenge to the appellate court's ruling in *Coalition for Economic Equity*, thereby leaving the Ninth Circuit's ruling in place and paving the way for the enforcement of Proposition 209.[8]

Notwithstanding the legal challenges and the Ninth Circuit's decision in *Coalition for Economic Equity*, city, county, and state agencies in California continue to rely on affirmative action to promote diversity.[9] The only way to enforce Proposition 209, seemingly, is to file a lawsuit against the government employer that continues to rely on affirmative action. However, there have been very few of such lawsuits[10] because law firms are reluctant to take on these cases, claiming that they are difficult to win and prone to summary judgments. In any event, whether to achieve diversity or to stave off employment discrimination suits by

women or people of color, government agencies in California are not willing to abolish their long-standing affirmative action programs. Because of
the mercurial nature of court decisions around affirmative action, it may
be the case in general that public sector employers are not willing to
abandon the affirmative action programs that have taken them decades
to institute. As will be seen in the following chapters, public and private
sector employers continue to rely on a host of tools and techniques,
including affirmative action, to redress employment discrimination and
to *diversify* their workforces.

Notes

1. See David H. Rosenbloom and Jay M. Shafritz, *Essentials of Labor Relations*
(Reston, Va.: Reston, 1985).

2. The circumstances would certainly dictate which legal mechanism would
apply. For example, it is now generally accepted that Section 1981 is not applicable to discrimination based on gender.

3. For a review of the legal history of affirmative action, see, for example,
Norma M. Riccucci, "The Legal Status of Affirmative Action," *Review of Public
Personnel Administration* 17 (1997): 22–37; and Riccucci, "Will Affirmative Action
Survive into the Twenty-First Century?" in Carolyn Ban and Norma M. Riccucci,
eds., *Public Personnel Management: Current Concerns, Future Challenges*, 2d ed.
(New York: Longman, 1997), pp. 57–72.

4. There are a number of other federal district and appellate court cases addressing affirmative action. As of this writing, they are pending, being argued, or have
not been (and perhaps will not be) appealed to the U.S. Supreme Court. Such cases
are not addressed in this chapter. See, for example, *Gratz and Hamacher v. Bollinger,
Duderstadt, and the Board of Regents of the University of Michigan* (2000), where a federal district court in Detroit upheld the University of Michigan's affirmative action
program on the grounds that racial preferences in admissions enhance the educational experience of not only people of color but whites as well. Yet a different
judge on that same federal district court in Detroit, in *Grutter v. the University of
Michigan Law School* (2001), struck down a race-conscious admissions program at
Michigan's law school as being unconstitutional. Also see *Majeske v. City of Chicago*
(2000), where the Court of Appeals for the Seventh Circuit struck down a reverse
discrimination suit by white police officers in the Chicago police department.

5. The *Hopwood* appellate court ruled that the law school's affirmative action
program could not meet the first prong of the strict scrutiny test. Strict scrutiny is
a two-pronged test that asks (1) whether there is a compelling governmental
interest for the program (e.g., to redress past discrimination) and (2) whether the
program is sufficiently narrowly tailored to meet its specified goals (e.g., whether
there are alternative programs that could be employed that do not classify people
by, for instance, race). Because the *Hopwood* court said the law school didn't meet
the first prong of the test, it went on to say, it did not need to apply the second
prong of the strict scrutiny test (*Hopwood,* 1996 at p. 955).

6. *Piscataway Township Board of Education v. Taxman*, 521 U.S. 1117; 117 S.Ct. 2506 (1997), cert. granted.

7. See, for example, David H. Rosenbloom, *Public Administration and Law* (New York: Marcel Dekker, 1983); and David H. Rosenbloom, "Public Employees' Liability for Constitutional Torts," in Carolyn Ban and Norma M. Riccucci, eds., *Public Personnel Management: Current Concerns, Future Challenges*, 2d ed. (New York: Longman, 1997), pp. 237–252.

8. See http://www.ci.sf.ca.us/cityattorney/prop209/prop209.htm. It should further be noted that the California courts have not yet ruled on whether Proposition 209 is valid under the U.S. Constitution.

9. See "Plaintive About Prop 209," *Recorder* online, December 5, 1997; available at http://web.lexis-nexis.com.

10. In one court case, *Cheresnik v. City and County of San Francisco* (1999), the Pacific Legal Foundation filed suit against the San Francisco International Airport on behalf of three white males who alleged they were denied a chance for promotions because of the airport's diversity plan. The leadership at San Francisco's airport remains committed to diversity and was unwilling to scrap its plan, despite Proposition 209. As of this writing, the case is pending in the San Mateo County Superior Court. In another case, *Schindler Elevator Corp. v. City and County of San Francisco* (1999), a company's bid for a city contract was rejected because it had not demonstrated good faith outreach efforts to minority subcontractors as required under San Francisco's Minority Business Enterprise/Women's Business Enterprise (MBE/WBE) ordinance. The company sued, asserting the MBE/WBE outreach provision violated Proposition 209. The case was decided on appeal in May 1999 in the city's favor. The court based its decision on contracting principles and did not reach the Proposition 209 issues.

Additional Reading

Cayer, N. Joseph. *Public Personnel Administration in the United States.* 3d ed. New York: St. Martin's, 1996.

"Civil Rights Act of 1991: Text and Analysis." *Employment Guide.* Special Supplement 6, no. 23 (1991). Washington, D.C.: Bureau of National Affairs.

Elliot, Robert H. "Human Resources Management's Role in the Future Aging of the Workforce." *Review of Public Personnel Administration*, Spring 1995. Symposium.

Guy, Mary E. "Public Personnel and Gender." *Review of Public Personnel Administration* Winter, 1996. Symposium.

Kellough, J. Edward. "The Supreme Court, Affirmative Action, and Public Management: Where Do We Stand Today?" *American Review of Public Administration* 21 (1991): 255–269.

Kellough, J. Edward, Sally Coleman Selden, and Jerome S. Legge Jr. "Affirmative Action Under Fire: The Current Controversy and the Potential for State Policy Retrenchment." *Review of Public Personnel Administration*, Fall 1997, pp. 52–74.

Ospina, Sonia M. *Illusions of Opportunity: Employee Expectations and Workplace Inequality.* Ithaca, N.Y.: Cornell University Press, 1996.

Rosenbloom, David H. *Federal Equal Employment Opportunity.* New York: Praeger, 1977.

Selden, Sally Coleman. *The Promise of Representative Bureaucracy.* Armonk, N.Y.: Sharpe, 1997.

Slack, James D. "The Americans with Disabilities Act and the Workplace: Observations About Management's Responsibilities in AIDS-Related Situations." *Public Administration Review,* July-August 1995, pp. 365–370.

Cases

Adarand v. Peña, 115 5. Ct 2097 (1995).

Cheresnik v. City and County of San Francisco, 99-4109 (1999).

Claus v. Duquesne Light Company, 46 F. 3d 1115 (3rd Cir. 1994, unpublished opinion), *cert. denied,* 115 5. Ct. 1700 (1995).

Coalition for Economic Equity v. Pete Wilson, 946 F. Supp. 1480 (1996); *vacated and remanded,* 122 F.3d. 692 (1997); *cert. denied,* 522 U.S. 963 (1997).

Fullilove v. Klutznick, 448 U.S. 448 (1980).

Gratz and Hamacher v. Bollinger, Duderstadt, and the Board of Regents of the University of Michigan, 97-CV-75231-DT (December 13, 2000).

Grutter v. the University of Michigan Law School, 97-CV-75928-DT (March 27, 2001).

Hopwood v. State of Texas, 861 F. Supp. 551 W.D. Tex. (1994); *rev'd and remanded in part, diss'd in part,* 78 F. 3d. 932 (5th Cir. 1996); *cert. denied,* 518 U.S. 1033 (1996).

In re Birmingham Reverse Discrimination Employment Litigation (BRDEL), 20 F. 3d. 1525 (11th Cir. 1994), *cert. denied sub nom. Martin V. Wilks,* 115 5. Ct. 1965 (1995).

Int'l Assoc. of Firefighters v. City of Cleveland, 478 U.S. 501 (1986).

Johnson v. Transportation Agency of Santa Clara County, 480 U.S. 624 (1987).

Lesage v. Texas, A-96-CA-286 (unpublished) (1997); *rev'd,* 158 F.3d 213 (1998); *rev'd and remanded,* 120 S. Ct. 467 (1999).

Majeske v. City of Chicago, 2000 U.S. App. LEXIS 15839 (3d Cir. 2000).

Martin v. Wilks, 490 U.S. 755 (1989).

Firefighters Local Union and Memphis Fire Department v. Stotts, 104 S. Ct. 582 (1984).

Metro Broadcasting v. F.C.C., 111 L. Ed. 2d 445 (June 27, 1990).

Piscataway Township Board of Education v. Taxman. See *Taxman v. Piscataway.*

Regents v. Bakke, 438 U.S. 265 (1978).

Richmond v. Croson, 488 U.S. 469 (1989).

Schindler Elevator Corp. v. City and County of San Francisco, A081811 (unpublished) San Francisco County Super. Ct. no. 991956 (1999).

Sheet Metal Workers' International Association v. EEOC, 478 U.S. 421 (1986).

Smith v. University of Washington, 2 F. Supp. 2d 1324 (W.D. Wash. 1998); *aff'd,* 233 F.3d 1188 (9th Cir. 2000).

United Steelworkers v. Weber, 443 U.S. 193 (1979).

Taxman v. Piscataway Township Board of Education, 798 F. Supp. 1093 (1992); 832 F. Supp. 836 (1993); 91 F.3d 1547 (1996); *Piscataway Township Board of Education v. Taxman,* 521 U.S. 1117; 117 S. Ct. 2506 (1997), *cert. granted.*

Wygant v. Jackson Bd of Ed., 476 U.S. 267 (1986).

3

Initial Steps in Preparing for Diversity in the Workplace

In the last decade or so, many organizations have been going to great lengths to prepare for and manage diverse workforces as a matter of competitive survival. But there is an underlying reason why "managing diversity" continues to merit a good deal of energy and resources: race, ethnicity, and gender, among others, remain heated issues in our society. Although progress has been made toward combating employment discrimination, discriminatory practices in the workplace as well as *perceptions* of bias and discrimination continue to exist (see Tables 3.1, 3.2). Moreover, other, more subtle forms of bias and discrimination are also present in the workplace. They are manifested in large part as negative attitudes and behaviors toward differences. Quite simply, human beings often react disparagingly to the fact that all people do not look alike, dress alike, talk alike, or think alike. In effect, as traditional, homogeneous workforces become increasingly diverse, tensions in the workplace are inevitable.

These tensions, along with efforts to ameliorate them, are certainly not unique to the work setting. Many universities across the country require students to take either a racial or a cultural diversity course in their first year of study, or to participate in "diversity" workshops during the orientation for new students. For example, some universities run all-male discussion groups on "acquaintance" or "date" rape. Other universities show videos to their incoming students that address such topics as race relations on university campuses. The point is that efforts to prepare environments for diversity is given priority status by major institutions across America.

TABLE 3.1　Charges of Discrimination Filed with the Equal Employment Opportunity Commission (EEOC), 1992–2000

	FY 1992	FY 1993	FY 1994	FY 1995	FY 1996	FY 1997	FY 1998	FY 1999	FY 2000
Total charges	72,302	87,942	91.189	87,529	77,990	80,680	79,591	77,444	79,896
Race	29,548	31,695	31.656	29,986	26,287	29,199	28.820	28,819	28,945
	40.9%	36.0%	34.8%	34.3%	33.8%	36.2%	36.2%	37.3%	36.2%
Sex	27,796	23,919	25,860	26,181	23,813	24,728	24,454	23,907	25,194
	30.1%	27.2%	28.4%	29.9%	30.6%	30.7%	30.7%	30.9%	31.5%
National Origin	7,434	7,454	7,414	7,035	6,687	6,712	6,778	7,108	7,792
	10.3%	8.5%	8.1%	8.0%	8.6%	8.3%	8.5%	9.2%	9.8%
Religion	1,388	1,449	1,546	1,581	1,564	1,709	1,786	1,811	1,939
	1.9%	1.6%	1.7%	1.8%	2.0%	2.1%	2.2%	2.3%	2.4%
Retaliation									
All statutes	11,096	13,814	15,853	17,070	16,080	18,198	19,114	19,694	21,613
	15.3%	15.7%	17.4%	19.5%	20.6%	22.6%	24.0%	25.4%	27.1%
Title VII	10,499	12,644	14,415	15,342	14,412	16,394	17,246	11,883	19,753
	14.5%	14.4%	15.8%	17.5%	18.5%	20.3%	21.7%	23.1%	24.7%
Age	19,573	19,809	19,618	17,416	15,719	15,785	15,191	14,141	16,008
	27.1%	22.5%	21.5%	19.9%	20.2%	19.6%	19.1%	18.3%	20.0%
Disability	1,048[a]	15,274	18,859	19,798	18,046	18,108	17,806	17,007	15,864
	1.4%	17.4%	20.7%	22.6%	23.1%	22.4%	22.4%	22.0%	19.9%
Equal Pay Act	1,294	1,328	1,381	1,275	969	1,134	1,071	1,044	1,270
	1.8%	1.5%	1.5%	1.5%	1.2%	1.4%	1.3%	1.3%	1.6%

Notes: [a]Only partial data available, since the Americans with Disabilities Act became effective in July 1992.

Source: U.S. Equal Employment Opportunity Commission (EEOC), www.eeoc.gov.

As noted in Chapter 1, race, ethnicity, and gender are the most critical dimensions of diversity. They are perhaps key in how we identify and process differences and, ultimately, in how we shape and form our worldviews. As Marilyn Loden and Judy Rosener[1] point out, race, ethnicity, and gender, as well as age, physical ability, and sexual orientation, are *primary* dimensions of diversity, in that they represent individual characteristics or factors that *cannot* be changed. (Admittedly, gender can

TABLE 3.2   Equal Employment Opportunity Commission (EEOC) Litigation Statistics, 1992–1999

	FY92	FY93	FY94	FY95	FY96	FY97	FY98	FY99
All suits filed	447	481	425	373	193	338	405	465
Direct suits	347	398	357	328	167	305	366	439
Title VII	242	260	235	193	106	175	229	324
ADA	NA[a]	3	34	81	38	80	79	54
ADEA[b]	84	115	74	41	13	36	36	40
EPA[c]	2	2	0	1	1	0	2	4
Concurrent	19	18	14	12	9	14	20	17

Notes: [a] The Americans with Disabilities Act became effective in July 1992.
[b] The Age Discrimination in Employment Act of 1967.
[c] The Equal Pay Act of 1963.

Source: U.S. Equal Employment Opportunity Commission (EEOC), www.eeoc.gov.

be altered surgically but for purposes of this discussion it is considered a primary dimension.) These core characteristics of diversity significantly affect the attitudes and behaviors of individuals and groups in our society. They are the essence of our existence and affect how we perceive and respond to those who do not share our own individual characteristics.

The *secondary* dimensions of diversity, which Loden and Rosener define as malleable factors such as educational background, geographic location, income, marital status, parental status, and religion, can also influence our attitudes and behaviors toward others (see Figure 3.1). For example, single women may perceive married women as less committed to their careers; persons with lower incomes may be looked down on by persons with higher incomes; persons with higher levels of education may view themselves as superior to those with less education; persons from the South may view persons from the Northeast as snobby "blue-bloods," while northeasterners may view southerners as slow and dumb. Although these factors can give rise to tensions in the workplace, they do not tend to engender the enmity and hatred that have historically been generated by the primary dimensions of diversity. (The one exception may be religion, although religious divisiveness and its ensuing turmoil are more pervasive outside the United States.) Subsequent chapters in this book, therefore, will focus on the primary dimensions of diversity.

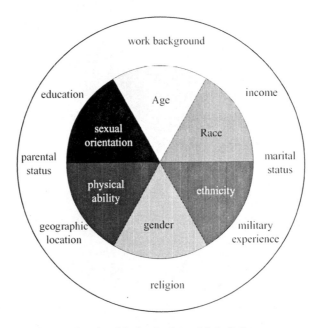

Source: Based on Marilyn Loden and Judy B. Rosener,
Workforce America! (Homewood, Ill.: Business One
Irwin, 1991).

FIGURE 3.1   Primary and Secondary Dimensions of Diversity

Setting the Stage

Public policy analysts and researchers have submitted that one of the most important ingredients to setting up successful diversity programs is strong commitment from not only agency leaders but also CEOs, such as mayors, governors, and the president.[2] If top-level leaders communicate that a program to manage diversity is a critical goal for the agency and that it is *integrated into the overall strategic goals* of the organization, the stage is set for commitment by lower-level managers, supervisors, and the employees themselves. Leaders' expressions of commitment, however, must be backed by resources. Adequate resources in the form of both funding and staff are essential to achieving diversity goals. But more than this, if top-level leaders are genuinely committed to diversity objectives, the persons responsible for implementing the diversity programs must be held accountable for goal attainment. In other words, to the extent that managing diversity is a priority for the agency, it should be afforded the same weight as other important organizational goals. In this sense, managers and supervisors would be held accountable for reaching the diversity goals.

One of the most important areas that must be targeted for generous funding is training. Training is generally relegated to a back burner during fiscal crises, but keeping training as a primary activity will ensure that efforts to manage diversity are successful. Training programs and policies are crucial to fostering multicultural awareness among managers, supervisors, and employees, instilling a sense of value around diversity and improving the overall management of diversity in the workplace.

The success of training programs may lie in the organization's ability to target the programs and policies to specific organizational needs. For example, if the organization is faced with an aging workforce, then training would, in part, be geared toward dispelling myths around older workers.

It is essential that a sense of "ownership" be instilled in managers and supervisors as well as employees. Because everyone in the workplace represents a challenge to successfully managing diversity, everyone must be involved, to varying degrees and capacities, in developing ways to effectively manage diversity in the workforce. This may ultimately foster greater and *shared* commitment to achieving the diversity goals.

Organizations must assess and understand the current demographic complexion of their workforce and, in conjunction with projected forecasts for change, develop workforce planning models to target areas for recruitment, hiring, training, and retention. Such planning will not only help determine skills' gaps and targets of opportunity, but it will also help management in the allocation of agency resources so that a high-quality workforce is ultimately realized.

In addition, assessing the cultural environment of the existing workforce can identify challenges and barriers to successfully managing diversity. The U.S. Office of Personnel Management (OPM), which is responsible for the management of personnel and human resources at the federal level of government, suggests the use of "cultural audits" or "organizational needs assessments." These are surveys distributed to employees to assess their views on diversity; the feedback can help the agency target potential strengths and weaknesses in its efforts to manage diversity.

Golembiewski[3] makes the important point that traditional, bureaucratic infrastructures serve as major impediments to successful diversity programs. As he and other organizational theorists have repeatedly told us, the culture of organizations tends to be male, white, and Eurocentric in orientation. This is due mainly to the fact that the culture of organizations reflects those who run and control them. It is axiomatic that such a culture will work against efforts to manage diversity.[4]

An organization culture that supports flexibility is necessary so that supervisors can manage effectively in a diverse environment. Governments must make efforts to modify organizational policies (written and unwritten) to incorporate the cultural perspectives of those other than the majority group. Although it is impossible to consider every situation and policy that may have an adverse effect on women, people of color, the disabled, and older workers, recognizing the existence of views in the workforce other than those commonly held by white males, will allow managers and workers to be more productive. In other words, in a culturally diverse workforce, there cannot be "one best way" to manage; management styles will depend on the workplace over which a supervisor is responsible.

Government employers have been relying increasingly on the services of temporary employees to meet shifting workloads and, at the same time, strive to maintain continuous, effective services to the public. In the broader context of managing diversity, government employers need to ensure that they are effectively managing the "contingent workforce" and the "indirect and alternative workforce," as the U.S. Bureau of Labor Statistics refers to workers without an employment contract and temporary workers, respectively. This is critical, especially since women and people of color, as *Workforce 2020* reports, represent relatively high concentrations in these jobs (see Table 3.3 for contingent workers in government).

Temporary employees work without any promise of permanent employment, and they also receive very few employee benefits. In the federal government, where the number of temporary employees ranges from 7 to 10 percent,[5] agencies are permitted to extend temporary appointments in one-year increments, up to a total of four years for any given temporary employee. (In reality, research has shown that temporary appointments can last up to ten years or more.[6]) It is important for government employers to ensure that these workers are not abused, since their merit protections are limited as temporary workers. And, as the U.S. Office of Personnel Management (OPM) points out, "Employees who believe they are being treated unfairly are likely to evidence a lower com-

TABLE 3.3   Percentage of Contingent Workers in Government, by Gender and Race, 1995

	Contingent Workers
Total	2.7 [a]
Men	0.6
Women	2.0
White	1.0
African American	1.8

Source: Calculated from tables in Anne E. Polivka, "A Profile of Contingent Workers." *Monthly Labor Review A2* (October), 1996, pp. 10-21.

[a]Polivka estimates that in February of 1995, there were 2.7 million contingent workers in the United States. This estimate is restricted to wage and salary workers who expected their jobs to last for an additional year or less and who had worked their jobs for one year or less. As noted above, 2.7 percent, or 72,900, contingent employees worked in government occupations. This figure does not include temporary workers.

mitment to the job and their employers—the American public."[7] Government employers must also seek to minimize conflicts between full-time permanent workers and part-timers. The reliance on temporary workers limits the potential job and promotion opportunities for full-time workers. Moreover, employers are able to convert temporary employees to permanent status, which can also threaten the job opportunities and status of full-time job incumbents. Whether or not race and gender conflicts are also imminent here, government employers would find it in their best interest to manage the contingent and alternative workforce in order to maintain harmony in the workplace and ultimately efficient and effective service provision to the American people.

Finally, it is critical to point out that public sector organizations that perfunctorily develop diversity programs solely for the purpose of avoiding liability in potential lawsuits completely miss the point about the importance of diversity programs. Moreover, they will fail to adequately plan for their own successful performance, as well as the future governance of the American people. So too will organizations that simply rename or relabel their old affirmative action programs as "managing diversity" programs.

In sum, there are several initial steps for public sector organizations to take in order to prepare for the development and implementation of diversity programs. These steps are critical for *all* the primary dimensions of diversity. Beyond these initial measures, the various management strategies embraced by agencies in organizing and developing diversity programs must obviously be geared toward each of the specified dimensions of diversity—race, ethnicity, gender, physical ability, age, and sex-ual orientation. The following chapters are thus organized around diversity issues and strategies aimed at the primary dimensions of diversity.

Notes

1. Marilyn Loden and Judy B. Rosener, *Workforce America!* (Homewood, Ill.: Business One Irwin, 1991).

2. See, for example, the survey results administered to sixty-five public and private sector organizations by a task force of Vice President Gore's National Partnership for Reinventing Government (Best Practices in Achieving Workforce Diversity, 2000). Also see Sonia M. Ospina, "Realizing the Promise of Diversity," in James L. Perry, ed., *Handbook of Public Administration,* 2d ed. (San Francisco: Jossey-Bass, 1996).

3. Robert T. Golembiewski, *Managing Diversity in Organizations* (Tuscaloosa: University of Alabama Press, 1995).

4. Also see Ospina, "Realizing the Promise."

5. See www.opm.gov.

6. See U.S. Office of Personnel Management (OPM), *Temporary Federal Employment* (Washington, D.C.: OPM, 1994).

7. Ibid., p. ix.

Additional Reading

Best Practices in Achieving Workforce Diversity. Washington, D.C.: U.S. Department of Commerce and the National Partnership for Reinventing Government Benchmarking Study, October 2000.

Broadnax, Walter D., ed. *Diversity and Affirmative Action in Public Service.* Boulder: Westview, 2000.

Civil Service 2000. Indianapolis: Hudson Institute, June 1988.

Copeland, Lennie. "Valuing Diversity, Part 1: Making the Most of Cultural Differences at the Workplace." *Personnel,* June 1988, pp. 52–60.

Guajardo, Salomon A. "Workforce Diversity: Monitoring Employment Trends in Public Organizations." *Public Personnel Management,* Spring 1999, pp. 63–86.

Fullerton, Howard N., Jr. "New Labor Force Projections, Spanning 1988 to 2000." *Outlook 2000,* U.S. Department of Labor, April 1990, pp. 1–11.

Golembiewski, Robert T. *Managing Diversity in Organizations.* Tuscaloosa: University of Alabama Press, 1995.

Hopkins, Willie E., Karen Sterkel-Powell, and Shirley A. Hopkins. "Training Priorities for a Diverse Workforce." *Public Personnel Management*, Fall 1994, pp. 429–435.

Kellough, J. Edward and Katherine C. Naff. "Managing Diversity in the Federal Service." Paper presented at the Sixth National Public Management Conference, 2001, Bloomington, Indiana.

Laudicina, Eleanor V. "Managing Workforce Diversity in Government: An Initial Assessment." *Public Administration Quarterly* 19 (1995): 170–192.

Loden, Marilyn, and Judy B. Rosener. *Workforce America!* Homewood, Ill.: Business One Irwin, 1991.

Mathews, Audrey. "Diversity: A Principle of Human Resource Management." *Public Personnel Management*, Summer 1998, pp. 175–186.

Meeting Public Demands: Federal Services in the Year 2000. U.S. Treasury Department, 1988.

Naff, Katharine C. *To Look Like America: Dismantling Barriers for Women and Minorities in Government.* Boulder: Westview, 2001.

Offermann, Lynn R., and Marilyn K. Gowing. "Organizations of the Future." *American Psychologist* 45 (1990): 134–143.

Opportunity 2000: Creative Affirmative Action Strategies for a Changing Workforce. Indianapolis: Hudson Institute, September 1988.

Ospina, Sonia M. *Illusions of Opportunity: Employee Expectations and Workplace Inequality.* Ithaca, N.Y.: Cornell University Press, 1996.

Riccucci, Norma M., and Tamu Chambers. "Models of Excellence in Workplace Diversity." In Carolyn Ban and Norma Riccucci, eds., *Public Personnel Management: Current Concerns, Future Challenges*, pp. 73–90. 2d ed. New York: Longman, 1997.

Rubaii-Barrett, Nadia, and Ann C. Beck. "Minorities in the Majority. Implications for Managing Cultural Diversity." *Public Personnel Management*, Winter 1993, pp. 503–521.

Soni, Vidu. "A Twenty-First Century Reception for Diversity in the Public Sector: A Case Study." *Public Administration Review*, September-October 2000, pp. 395–408.

U.S. Office of Personnel Management. *Building and Maintaining a Diverse, High-Quality Workforce.* Washington, D.C., June 2000.

Wilson, Elisabeth M., and Paul A. Iles. "Managing Diversity: An Employment and Service Delivery Challenge," *International Journal of Public Sector Management* 12 (1999): 27–48.

Wise, Lois Recascino, and Mary Tschirhart. "Examining Empirical Evidence on Diversity Effects: How Useful Is Diversity Research for Public-Sector Managers." *Public Administration Review*, September-October 2000, pp. 386–394.

Wise, Lois Recascino, Mary Tschirhart, Deborah K. Hosinski, and Lana Bandy. *Diversity Research: A Meta-Analysis.* Stockholm, Sweden: Institute for Future Studies, 1997.

Wooldridge, Blue; Barbara Clark Maddox; and Yan Zhang. "Changing Demographics of the Work Force: Implications for the Design of Productive

Work Environments: An Exploratory Analysis." *Review of Public Personnel Administration*, 15, 1995, pp. 60–72.

Wooldridge, Blue and Jennifer Wester. "The Turbulent Environment of Public Personnel Administration: Responding to the Challenge of Changing Workplace of the Twenty-First Century." Public Personnel Management, 40, 199, pp. 207–224.

Workforce 2000. Indianapolis: Hudson Institute, 1987.

Workforce 2020. Indianapolis: Hudson Institute, 1997.

4

Race, Ethnicity, and Diversity Management

One of the front-page headlines in a July 2000 *New York Times* article was "Nooses, Symbols of Race Hatred, at Center of Workplace Lawsuits."[1] For some, such an image might seem so arcane, hateful, and anachronistic that it couldn't possibly be true in today's work setting. For others, it is a reality that must be endured even as we enter the new millennium. Although this may be an extreme example, racism remains an insidious problem in our society, with deep social, political, and institutional roots. Diversity programs certainly cannot ameliorate the pervasive plight of racism in our society, but they can help make the workplace a less hostile, more accommodating, and healthier setting for all its members.

This chapter will address strategies for combating racism and other related, pernicious problems in the workplace, with the ultimate goal of making a diverse work environment more conducive to productive, fulfilled workers. But first, a snapshot of the trends in the status of public sector workforces is in order. As noted in the previous chapter, an inventory of an organization's current demographic complexion, including the job status of people of color, is the logical starting point for developing diversity programs.

The Racial and Ethnic Mix of Workers in Public Employment

Tables 4.1 and 4.2 show that there has been an increase in the percentages of people of color in the federal, state, and local government workforces. In

TABLE 4.1   Federal Executive Branch (Non-postal) Employment, by Race and Ethnicity, 1986–1998

	1986	1988	1990	1992	1996	1998
TOTAL	2,083,985	2,125,148	2,150,359	2,175,715	1,890,406	1,804,591
RACE/ETHNICITY						
Non minority	1,542,203	1,557,793	1,562,846	1,570,812	1,341,157	1,268,790
% Non minority	74.0	73.3	72.7	72.2	70.9	70.3
Total minorities	541,782	567,355	587,513	604,903	549,249	534,801
% Minority	26.0	26.7	27.3	27.8	29.1	29.6
African American	339,770	350,052	356,867	360,725	313,810	300,661
% African American	16.3	16.5	16.6	16.6	16.6	16.7
Latino	105,191	109,566	115,170	120,296	115,644	115,545
% Latino	5.0	5.2	5.4	5.5	6.1	6.4
Asian/Pacific Islander	62,137	70,032	76,312	81,522	81,851	81,028
% Asian/Pacific Islander	3.0	3.3	3.5	3.7	4.3	4.5
American Indian/Alaska Native	34,684	37,705	39,164	42,360	37,944	37,567
% American Indian/Alaska Native	1.7	1.8	1.8	1.9	2.0	2.1

Source: U.S. Office of Personnel Management (OPM): www.opm.gov.

fact, a good deal of research has shown that people of color have made inroads into public sector employment, at least in terms of entry-level jobs.[2]

However, the research further shows that people of color continue to be concentrated in lower-level, lower-paying positions in government work-forces (see Tables 4.3, 4.4). As the tables show, higher-level professional jobs, which carry greater levels of authority as well as pay, are domi-nated by whites, while the lower-level jobs tend to be filled predomi-nately by people of color.

The research also shows that occupational segregation continues to exist, whereby people of color are in departments or agencies that have traditionally employed them (see tables 4.5, 4.6). For example, in the fed-eral service, people of color are concentrated in such agencies as Health and Human Services and Housing and Urban Development. Similarly, in state and local governments they are highly represented in such depart-ments or agencies as hospitals and sanatoriums, housing and sanitation. They are not highly concentrated in such departments as fire and finan-cial administration.

The statistics presented above point to at least three important mes-sages for the development of diversity management programs as they relate to persons of color. First, that government workforces are indeed

TABLE 4.2 State and Local Government Employment, by Race, Ethnicity, and Gender, 1985–1997 (Percentages)

	MEN		
	1985	1989	1997
TOTAL	2,789,174	3,030,166	2,897,947
Race/Ethnicity			
Non minority	73.6	72.4	70.6
Total minority male	13.2	13.8	14.6
African American	8.9	9.0	8.7
Latino	3.2	3.5	. 4.2
Asian/Pacific Islander	0.8	1.0	1.3
American Indian/ Alaska Native	.03	0.3	0.4

	WOMEN		
	1985	1989	1997
TOTAL	1,952,334	2,227,265	2,307,015
Race/Ethnicity			
Non minority	29.5	29.6	29.6
Total minority female	11.6	12.3	14.8
African American	8.7	9.3	10.0
Latino	2.0	2.0	3.3
Asian/Pacific Islander	0.7	0.9	1.2
American Indian/ Alaska Native	0.2	0.1	0.3

increasingly diverse and, as demographers have said, they will continue to become more diverse. Thus developing programs to manage and accommodate a diverse work environment is critical for effective governmental performance.

The statistics also suggest that government organizations must ensure that people of color have access to *all* departments and agencies. By allowing them to be segregated into certain departments, governments

TABLE 4.3 Federal Employment Trends by White-Collar Occupational Category (All Employees), 1986–1998

		Total		Nonminority		Minority		Black		Hispanic		Asian/Pacific Islander		American Indian/ Alaska Native	
		#	%	#	%	#	%	#	%	#	%	#	%	#	%
Professional	1986	388,367	100.0	329,768	84.9	58,599	15.1	24,799	6.4	11,801	3.0	18,456	4.8	3,543	0.9
	1996	459,121	100.0	365,522	79.6	93,599	20.4	36,352	7.9	18,708	4.1	32,920	7.2	5,619	1.2
	1998	439,041	100.0	345,566	78.7	93,475	21.3	35,973	8.2	18,548	4.2	33,111	7.5	5,843	1.3
Administrative	1986	472,990	100.0	385,396	81.5	87,594	18.5	55,048	11.6	19,059	4.0	8,380	1.8	5,107	1.1
	1996	528,238	100.0	404,448	76.6	123,790	23.4	72,129	13.7	30,083	5.7	14,354	2.7	7,224	1.4
	1998	530,192	100.0	400,234	75.5	129,958	24.5	75,274	14.2	31,946	6.0	15,176	2.9	7,562	1.4
Technical	1986	359,035	100.0	258,759	72.1	100,276	27.9	65,430	18.2	17,320	4.8	7,737	2.2	9,789	2.7
	1996	365,499	100.0	237,936	65.1	127,513	34.9	80,440	22.0	23,533	6.4	12,242	3.3	11,298	3.1
	1998	348,720	100.0	223,161	64.0	125,559	36.0	78,003	22.4	24,169	6.9	12,275	3.5	11,112	3.2
Clerical	1986	415,309	100.0	267,711	64.5	147,598	35.5	106,268	25.6	23,945	5.8	10,559	2.5	6,826	1.6
	1996	224,040	100.0	128,786	57.5	95,254	42.5	65,470	29.2	16,099	7.2	8,192	3.7	5,493	2.5
	1998	198,222	100.0	112,836	56.9	85,386	43.1	57,603	29.1	14,958	7.5	7,696	3.9	5,129	2.6
Other	1986	40,540	100.0	28,290	69.8	12,250	30.2	7,216	17.8	3,358	8.3	917	2.3	759	1.9
	1996	46,357	100.0	30,010	64.9	16,256	35.1	8,230	17.8	5,805	12.5	1,251	2.7	970	2.1
	1998	47,469	100.0	30,353	63.9	17,116	36.1	8,316	17.5	6,583	13.9	1,247	2.6	970	2.0
Total White Collar[a]	1986	1,676,241	100.0	1,269,924	75.8	406,317	24.2	258,761	15.4	75,483	4.5	46,049	2.7	26,024	1.6
	1996	1,623,205	100.0	1,166,793	71.9	456,412	28.1	262,621	16.2	94,228	5.8	68,959	4.2	30,604	1.9
	1998	1,563,644	100.0	1,112,150	71.1	451,494	28.9	255,169	16.3	96,204	6.2	69,505	4.4	30,616	2.0

Note: [a]The total white-collar totals shown for 1986 do not include unspecified counts.
Source: U.S. Office of Personnel Management, Central Personnel Data File (CPDF).

TABLE 4.4 Employment of Protected-Class Persons by Occupation in State and Local Governments, 1985[a], 1989[b], 1997[c]

		Men				
	Year	Total Employment	Total Minority Male %	African American %	Latino %	Asian %	Native American %
Total (All occupations)	1985	2,789,174	13.2	8.9	3.2	0.8	0.3
	1989	3,030,166	13.8	9.0	3.5	1.0	0.3
	1997	2,897,947	14.6	8.7	4.2	1.3	0.4
Officials/Administrators	1985	181,284	7.2	4.3	1.9	0.7	0.3
	1989	202,644	7.9	4.9	2.0	0.8	0.2
	1997	197,497	9.5	5.5	2.6	1.1	0.3
Professionals	1985	506,823	7.8	4.1	1.9	1.6	0.2
	1989	583,307	4.5	2.1	1.8	0.2	0.2
	1997	605,274	9.5	4.7	2.5	2.1	0.2
Technicians	1985	285,374	9.4	5.4	2.7	1.0	0.3
	1989	297,913	10.9	6.2	3.2	1.2	0.3
	1997	265,326	12.2	6.3	3.9	1.6	0.4
Protective Service	1985	655,338	16.0	10.9	4.3	0.4	0.4
	1989	744,606	17.5	11.7	4.9	0.5	0.4
	1997	812,660	20.6	12.4	6.8	0.9	0.5
Paraprofessionals	1985	108,274	10.2	8.0	1.7	0.4	0.1
	1989	108,427	10.1	7.6	1.8	0.5	0.2
	1997	99,569	10.6	7.5	2.2	0.7	0.2
Office/Clerical/ Administrative Support	1985	107,002	3.4	2.4	0.9	0.4	0.1
	1989	119,477	4.0	2.4	1.0	0.5	0.1
	1997	116,502	4.8	2.6	1.4	0.7	0.1

TABLE 4.4 (continued)

Men

	Year	Total Employment	Total Minority Male %	African American %	Latino %	Asian %	Native American %
Skilled Craft	1985	382,311	20.2	12.7	5.9	0.9	0.7
	1989	424,617	21.2	13.1	6.2	1.2	0.7
	1997	384,868	23.9	14.0	7.5	1.6	0.8
Service/Maintenance	1985	562,768	31.6	23.7	6.9	0.6	0.4
	1989	549,175	32.7	23.9	7.6	0.8	0.4
	1997	416,251	33.1	22.6	8.7	1.2	0.6

Women

	Year	Total Employment	Total Female %	White %	African American %	Latina %	Asian %	Native American %
Total (All occupations)	1985	1,952,334	41.2	29.5	8.7	2.0	0.7	0.2
	1989	2,227,265	42.4	29.6	9.3	2.0	0.9	0.1
	1997	2,307,015	44.4	29.6	10.0	3.3	1.2	0.3
Officials/Administrators	1985	70,602	28.0	22.9	3.9	0.8	0.3	0.1
	1989	89,747	30.7	24.1	4.9	1.1	0.4	0.1
	1997	99,124	33.4	2.3	4.9	1.5	0.6	0.2
Professionals	1985	447,784	46.9	36.3	7.2	1.6	1.6	0.2
	1989	566,131	49.3	37.2	8.2	1.9	1.8	0.2
	1997	685,873	53.1	38.1	9.4	3.0	2.3	0.3
Technicians	1985	186,276	39.5	28.5	8.2	1.8	0.8	0.2
	1989	198,820	40.0	27.8	8.6	2.4	1.1	0.2
	1997	190,913	41.8	28.1	8.7	3.4	1.5	0.2

TABLE 4.4 (*continued*)

			Women				
	Year	Total Employment	Total Female %	White %	African American %	Latina %	Asian %	Native American %
Protective Service	1985	68,852	9.5	6.4	2.6	0.5	0	0.1
	1989	104,204	12.3	7.8	3.6	0.7	0.1	0.1
	1997	155,909	16.1	9.3	5.3	1.2	0.1	0.1
Paraprofessionals	1985	259,808	70.6	44.0	22.7	2.9	0.6	0.3
	1989	276,867	71.9	44.2	22.9	3.5	0.8	0.4
	1997	269,147	73.0	43.5	22.6	5.2	1.3	0.4
Office/Clerical	1985	767,246	87.8	64.7	15.9	5.4	1.3	0.4
	1989	834,938	87.5	62.4	16.9	6.1	1.6	0.4
	1997	765,193	86.8	58.4	17.8	8.0	2.0	0.5
Skilled Craft	1985	14,636	3.7	2.7	0.7	0.1	0	0
	1989	17,264	3.9	2.8	0.8	0.2	0	0
	1997	20,940	5.2	3.6	1.2	0.3	0.1	0
Service/Maintenance	1985	137,130	9.6	10.6	7.5	1.1	0.2	0.1
	1989	139,294	20.2	10.7	7.8	1.3	0.3	0.1
	1997	119,918	22.4	11.3	8.8	1.7	0.4	0.2

Notes:

[a] Calculated from unpublished EEOC report.

[b] U.S. Equal Employment Opportunity Commission, *Job Patterns for Minorities and Women in State and Local Governments, 1989,* Washington, D.C., 1990.

[c] U.S. Equal Employment Opportunity Commission, *Job Patterns for Minorities and Women in State and Local Governments, 1997,* Washington, D.C., 1998.

TABLE 4.5 Distribution of Employees in Federal Government, by Race, Ethnicity, and Agency, 1998 (Percentages; Women and Men of Color Combined)

Agency	Total People of Color	African American	Latino	Asian or Pacific Islander	American Indian or Alaska Native	White
Total Executive Branch	29.6	16.7	6.4	4.5	2.1	70.4
Agriculture	21.1	10.6	5.6	2.4	2.5	78.9
Commerce	27.5	18.3	3.4	5.6	0.6	72.5
Defense	26.7	14.2	6.2	5.2	1	73.3
Energy	21.8	11.5	5.2	3.8	1.3	78.2
Health & Human Services	41.5	16.7	2.9	5.1	16.9	58.5
Housing & Urban Development	45.0	34.0	6.7	3.2	1.1	55.0
Interior	26.8	5.5	4.3	1.6	15.4	73.2
Justice	31.9	16.2	12.2	2.8	0.8	68.1
Labor	34.4	24.3	6.6	2.9	0.7	65.6
State	23.3	14.9	4.2	3.7	0.4	76.7
Transportation	20.3	11.2	4.7	2.9	1.5	79.7
Treasury	34.2	21.7	8.4	3.3	0.8	65.8
Veterans Affairs	35.4	22.0	6.0	6.7	0.8	64.6

Source: U.S. Office of Personnel Management (OPM), www.opm.gov.

TABLE 4.6   Distribution of Employees in State and Local Governments, by Race, Ethnicity, and Selected Agencies, 1985, 1990, 1997

		White	African American	Latino	Asian American	American Indian
Financial	1985	78.2	13.7	5.4	2.2	0.5
administration	1990	74.2	16.5	6.3	2.6	0.4
	1997	72.5	15.9	7.8	3.3	0.5
Streets &	1985	81.2	12.2	4.6	1.3	0.7
highways	1990	79.8	12.7	5.0	1.8	0.7
	1997	78.0	12.6	6.1	2.4	0.9
Welfare	1985	67.0	25.1	6.0	1.4	0.5
	1990	63.6	26.1	7.6	2.2	0.6
	1997	60.4	25.3	10.8	2.8	0.7
Police	1985	81.8	12.0	5.1	0.7	0.4
	1990	78.3	14.0	6.2	1.0	0.4
	1997	72.7	16.1	9.0	1.7	0.5
Fire	1985	86.5	8.6	4.2	0.4	0.4
	1990	83.8	10.2	5.0	0.5	0.4
	1997	78.3	12.6	7.5	1.0	0.6
Hospitals &	1985	66.5	25.3	5.1	2.6	0.4
sanitoriums	1990	64.9	25.3	5.9	3.4	0.5
	1997	63.0	24.8	7.0	4.7	0.4
Health	1985	72.1	21.2	4.1	2.2	0.3
	1990	69.4	21.7	5.7	2.8	0.4
	1997	64.8	23.8	7.3	3.5	0.6
Housing	1985	49.9	37.6	10.6	1.4	0.4
	1990	49.0	37.0	11.4	2.3	0.4
	1997	45.6	39.5	11.1	3.3	0.5
Community	1985	77.7	14.6	5.0	2.2	0.4
development	1990	77.5	14.4	5.0	2.6	0.5
	1997	71.3	17.2	7.1	3.9	0.5
Corrections	1985	71.9	21.1	5.2	1.0	0.7
	1990	69.5	22.9	6.0	1.0	0.6
	1997	66.5	23.9	7.7	1.2	0.7
Sanitation	1985	59.5	31.7	7.4	1.0	0.4
	1990	58.6	30.7	8.4	1.8	0.5
	1997	54.8	31.9	9.8	2.9	0.6

Source: Job Patterns for Minorities and Women in State and Local Governments, 1985; *Job Patterns for Minorities and Women in State and Local Governments*, 1990; *Job Patterns for Minorities and Women in State and Local Governments*, 1997. Washington, D.C.: Equal Employment Opportunity Commission.

deprive all agencies and departments of the full benefits that diversity has to offer. And, as previously noted, diversity, and successfully managing it in the workplace, functions to ultimately improve the overall governance of society.

Finally, governments at all levels will need to place greater emphasis on the promotion opportunities offered and available to people of color. Organizations cannot expect to concentrate persons of color in lower-level, lower-paying jobs over time without ramifications. To the extent that they do, dissatisfaction as well as resentment and low morale will ensue in the workplace, thereby threatening to impede not just diversity efforts but overall organizational performance.

Strategies for Managing Diversity

There are a number of strategies that government employers may consider or are already employing in their efforts to manage diversity. Although the following list is certainly not exhaustive, it represents an important number of steps that organizations have taken or can take to effectively manage racially and ethnically diverse workforces. These strategies follow and conjoin with the efforts to "set the stage" as discussed in Chapter 3. As noted there, a number of preliminary steps (e.g., working to change existing organizational cultures) are essential in setting up diversity management programs. Although it is not feasible here to address the specific issues and problems that each racial and ethnic group may face, organizations must be vigilant of the fact that each racial and ethnic group has unique experiences, interests, and histories in the workforce. Sometimes interracial and interethnic rivalries exist in the workplace, where one group (e.g., African Americans) resents another group (e.g., Asians) over perceived disparities in employment opportunities. These concerns too must be considered in the development of diversity programs.

Increasing Promotion Opportunities for People of Color

Securing a job in the public sector generally entails passing a civil service or "merit" exam. Such exams can be oral, written, or a combination of both. They are referred to as "merit" exams because of the longstanding tradition in the public sector of hiring the best, "most qualified" workers for government jobs. However, a substantial body of research has shown that these exams have tended to adversely affect people of color.[3] They are often found to be culturally biased and related; they do not necessarily measure the actual requirements or qualifications for the job.[4] It was not uncommon at one time to take a civil service exam for an office job in the federal government and be asked, for example, such extraneous, irrelevant questions as, Which body of water does Florida fall in? Mitigating cultural biases does not simply denote developing the exams in, for example, Spanish or an Asian language. Rather, it suggests that efforts are made to ensure that *all* the job applicants are operating from a level, fair playing field (i.e., that they all approach the exam with the same level of skills, competencies, and education). Many communities, for example, have held training classes for people of color (but classes are open to everyone) interested in entering their police and fire departments. The training is intended to help potential job candidates prepare for the entry-level civil service exams, which generally include a written test and a physical agility test.

Federal, state, and local governments have made a good deal of progress in addressing the problem of discriminatory merit tests by reassessing job standards and requirements and, subsequently, redeveloping their civil service exams. However, many public employers have mainly targeted *entry-level* exams. But the problems persist in the promotion exams of many government workforces, thereby serving as a major obstacle to promotion opportunities for people of color.[5]

Thus it is important for government employers to ensure that their exams for promotion are accurate, fair, and job related. In addition, some government employers have provided training opportunities for *all* prospective candidates for promotion. Providing training so that all workers gain the work experience required for the higher-level jobs is an important way to assist people of color in their efforts to be promoted.[6] Sometimes providing tutoring or coaching on how to prepare for and take the test has proved very effective. Indeed, such methods have been successful in preparing persons of color for upper-level jobs in police and fire departments.

A survey conducted in June 2000 by the Merit Systems Protection Board (MSPB), the "watchdog" over the federal merit system, revealed that 54 percent of African American federal employees believe they are subjected to "flagrant or obviously discriminatory practices that hinder their career advancement" in the federal workplace. Interestingly enough, this finding from the 2000 survey is virtually the same as it was when the MSPB administered its survey in 1993.[7] The challenge for the federal government, then, is not only to develop a discrimination-free workplace but to cultivate agreement from all employees on what a discrimination-free workplace would look like and how it would operate so that career advancement opportunities are not—and are not perceived to be—inaccessible or closed to people of color. (These issues will be further addressed later in this chapter with the topic of training.)

Another impediment to the promotion of people of color is "moving the goalpost." This happens when employers continue to raise the qualifications for promotion, ultimately keeping people of color out of higher-level jobs. Typically, employees are told that they cannot advance to a higher post until they acquire a particular skill, such as obtaining a college degree or getting experience in another job function. When they achieve that goal, however, the employer then sets another requirement that puts the promotion further out of reach to the employee.[8] These sorts of practices tend to result in costly lawsuits, create serious tensions in the workplace, and negatively affect productivity. Government employers are challenged to ensure that such practices are not relied on in public sector workforces.

Experience and research further show that promotion opportunities are often made known via informal communications (e.g., word-of-mouth) or the "buddy" system. People of color have traditionally been kept out of these communication loops, often being bypassed all together. The ability of organizational leaders and managers to break down these circumscribed, "closed" communication systems and ensure that everyone has access to information about promotions is key.

Eradicating Racial Harassment

The "noose" incident described at the beginning of this chapter is perhaps one of the most violent and egregious representations of racial harassment because it is a reminder of the thousands of African Americans who died at the hands of lynch mobs in this country.[9] Although employment lawyers and analysts note that reports of nooses turning up in America's workplace are relatively rare, they do represent a portion of the growing number of racial harassment suits being brought against public and private sector organizations by African Americans, as well as Latinos, Asians, and American Indians.

Employment experts have surmised that the growing number of incidents of racial harassment in general reflect a backlash by white workers against affirmative action as well as an intolerance among younger workers who are uneducated about the civil rights struggles of the 1950s and 1960s and are fearful that affirmative action or diversity programs will hinder their own employment opportunities.

To compound the problem, victims of racial harassment have argued that when they inform their supervisors of the harassment, the supervisors either take no steps to redress or prevent the hostile conditions or they impede promotion opportunities and even fire employees for speaking out against racial harassment on the job. As noted in Chapter 3, organizational leaders are responsible for setting a tone of tolerance in the workplace and for ensuring that managers and supervisors don't ignore the grievances of employees who perceive they or others are being racially harassed. Managers and supervisors should be instructed to immediately investigate a charge of racial harassment, and organizations should hold them accountable for failing to do so.

It should be noted that an employer will obviously deny the existence of racial harassment in the face of a lawsuit filed by an alleged victim. The challenge for organizations is to *not reach* the point where there is even an opportunity for the occurrence of racial harassment (more on this will be discussed shortly under the topic of training).

As already noted, innumerable incidents of racial harassment continue to take place in the workplace, as indicated by the charges and lawsuits that are being filed against organizations. The Equal Employment Opportunity Commission (EEOC) reported that it received close to fifty thousand charges of racial harassment in the 1990s, compared with roughly ten thousand in the 1980s. A sampling of lawsuits, along with the charges involving racial harassment, illustrates the insidious nature of the problem:

Torres v. Pisano and New York University (1997).[10] At the time the suit was filed, Torres was employed as a secretary to Pisano at New York University's dental center. Torres alleged that Pisano habitually called her a "dumb cunt" or a "dumb spic." He frequently told her that she "should stay home, go on welfare, and collect food stamps like the rest of the spics."

Schwapp v. Town of Avon, Connecticut (1997).[11] In 1992 Schwapp was hired as the town's first African American police officer. He was

forced to resign two years later because of incessant, depreca-
tory harassment from his superiors and fellow police officers.
Some examples he gave included the continuous use of the term
"nigger" on the job; constantly being told that all the crimes in
Avon are committed by "niggers"; references to "nigger bitches"
in the community whom the police have to clean up after; and
disparaging remarks about African American football players
who do "that jungle dance every time they score a touchdown."

Richardson v. New York State Dept. of Correctional Service (1999).[12]
Richardson, an African American woman hired by the New York
State Department of Corrections as a clerk, charged that she was
subjected to a racially hostile work environment and that she was
retaliated against when she complained about and filed a lawsuit
to remedy that discrimination. Some of the racially hostile incidents she described include an anonymous person putting horse
manure in her parking spot and her supervisor referring to African American criminal suspects as "apes or baboons." Another
incident involved a coworker telling her, "all you spooks have a
nice Halloween." Her supervisor commented on pictures of
African American inmates, stating that "black people are so dark
you can't see them anyway," and terms such as "nigger" and
"Buckwheat" were used in reference to African Americans.

Robinson v. City and County of Denver (2000).[13] Robinson, an African-
American man, was employed as a first-level supervisor in the
city of Denver's Wastewater Management Division. The charges
stem from his being subjected to a racially hostile work environment and to disparate treatment because he is African American.
Some of the racially hostile actions he noted in his suit include a
derogatory letter taped on a wall near an elevator that was
addressed to all "dark-skinned people"; routinely finding racist
writings and graffiti on restroom walls, consisting of the words
"nigger" and "nigger lover" and drawings of a woman with
large breasts, a large posterior, and three African American men
with erections; a post-it note on a woman's lunch bag in the division's lunchroom refrigerator that said "Sucks Nigger Dicks."

This latter case is almost too egregious and offensive for print, but it is
offered as an illustration of the pervasive, hateful treatment that people
of color continue to be subjected to in the workplace. That public sector

organizations continue to allow such behavior to occur with impunity points to the dire need for diversity programs aimed at ridding the workplace of hostile, violent racial harassment.

Adhering to Affirmative Action Policy and Law

As noted in Chapter 2, a number of recent actions by the courts and citizen voter referenda have worked against affirmative action efforts in both the public and private sectors. Obviously it is critical to adhere to the law when developing diversity programs. However, organizations can certainly recast, modify, and repackage their programs, providing they operate within the parameters of the law. This is the case in California, as discussed in Chapter 2, where many communities in the state were unwilling to scrap their long-standing diversity programs after the voters of California passed Proposition 209 (this voter initiative abolished the use of affirmative action in public employment, public education, and public contracting). Recognizing the importance of successfully managing diversity, cities, towns, and counties across the state of California modified their diversity programs in order to maintain them.

Another example of how public sector employers respond to actions that might hinder efforts to promote diversity can be seen in the U.S. Supreme Court's 1989 decision, *City of Richmond v. Croson Company*, involving a "set-aside" program. This case involves Richmond's efforts to ensure diversity among the firms doing construction business with the city. In the early 1980s, the Richmond city council adopted a minority business enterprise (MBE) plan that required non–minority owned primary contractors of the city to subcontract at least 30 percent of the dollar amount of their contracts to MBEs. There was no geographic limit to the plan so that any MBE in the United States, providing the MBE was 51 percent owned and controlled by minority group members, was eligible for the 30 percent set-aside.

Upon challenge by a white-owned firm, the J.A. Croson Company, the U.S. Supreme Court struck down Richmond's set-aside program for minority-owned businesses. A number of cities across the country responded by immediately canceling or suspending their set-aside programs. Seattle was one city among many that was unwilling to do so. Rather, the city reassessed and adjusted its program in light of court-implied guidelines, which essentially said that a set-aside program must seek to rectify past discrimination by the city and must be narrowly tailored to achieve its intended purpose (i.e., if it intends to redress discrimination against African Americans, then the set-aside program should be aimed at African Americans in Richmond and not other groups from other geographic locations). In effect, the women- and minority-owned business enterprise programs continue to operate in Seattle as well as in a number of other jurisdictions across the country. This type of creative action is essential if government employers wish to maintain their affirmative action and diversity programs.

Some communities are offering training programs to help minority-owned businesses learn the cryptic terminology and language sometimes referred to as government contractese in order to secure contracts awarded by federal, state, and local governments. For example, the New York City Metropolitan Transit Authority, in conjunction with LaGuardia Community College and PricewaterhouseCoopers, offers a four-day course, PREP (Preparing for Profit), which is open to all small businesses but is particularly geared toward women- and minority-owned businesses. PREP helps clarify dense government rules and regulations and trains participants on how to cut through the profuse paperwork required for securing a government contract.

Training and Development

Perhaps the key to preparing managers, supervisors, and workers for diversity in the workforce lies in training, development, and education. Managers and supervisors, for example, will need to possess the tools and skills necessary to address and respond to changes in the demography of workplace (e.g., being attuned to the different values and expectations of various groups is critical).

As noted earlier, changing the culture of organizations is a key first step to managing diversity, so that diversity is supported and valued. Managers and supervisors will need to be trained to learn and understand the culture of the organization and the rules, values, and attitudes that undergird it. Ultimately, managers must be able to provide people of color with the information, knowledge, and tools they need for career advancement and job success.

Training and Development in Technology. *The Workforce 2000* reports urged employers, indeed the American society, to prepare for a technological revolution in the twenty-first century. Demographers and employment experts as a corollary have argued that American workers, in particular women and people of color, should be trained and educated in the new technologies needed to perform the new jobs. Advances in communications, information management, and biotechnologies along with the continuing shift of production from goods to services and the continued trends toward globalization have led to a *digital* revolution, resulting in dramatic changes to the nature of work in our society.

It is unclear whether or not government has effectively prepared people of color for these new jobs. However, research does tell us that educational policies continue to generate significant disparities between people of color and whites. The *Workforce 2020* report, for example, states that

> even though all American students need to learn more, it is minority students in particular whose futures are at greatest risk because they are inadequately educated. Thus educational improvement is particularly pressing for them.[14]

The report concludes that "the single most important goal of workforce development must be to improve the quality of American public education substantially."[15]

Admittedly, it is the American educational system, and not government employers, that bears the biggest responsibility for educating people of color for the economic realities ahead. Changing the nation's educational system goes beyond the scope of this book, but on-the-job training in positions that call for technology skills should not be overlooked as a viable way to ensure that people of color can fill the jobs of today and tomorrow. Otherwise the nation will continually import labor from abroad to fulfill its labor needs in the area of high-tech jobs (discussed later in this chapter in the context of immigrants).

Training to Combat Negative Stereotypes. Table 4.7 provides a list of commonly held stereotypes surrounding race and ethnicity. As the table indicates, anyone and everyone can possess negative stereotypes toward others, which constitute one of the most serious impediments to harmony in the workplace. They certainly highlight the fact that differences are treated with suspicion, mistrust, and disdain.

Government employers interested in creating healthy, productive workforces will need to develop training programs aimed at combating

TABLE 4.7   Commonly Held Racial and Ethnic Stereotypes

Group	Attributes
African Americans	Good athletes and great lovers; lazy; militant and violent; talk funny; unintelligent
Native Americans	Dishonest; drink too much; noble savages; oil tycoons and land barons; squaws, bucks, and Tonto
Asian Americans and Asians	All have same cultural heritage; xenophobes; secretive and sneaky; stoics; taking over America
European American	White only; no ethnic heritage; arrogant; insensitive; enemy of the oppressed; can't be trusted
Latino/Chicano/ Hispanic	Have same cultural heritage; macho men and subservient women; volatile and emotional; lazy; have big families
Pacific Islanders	Primitive; oversexed; ignorant and happy; childlike; gullible

Source: Adapted from Marilyn Loden and Judy B. Rosener *Workforce America!* Homewood, Ill.: Business One Irwin (1991).

the negative attitudes and stereotypes that managers and workers have toward people of color. These negative attitudes represent a major deterrent to successfully managing diversity in the workforce.

Some public and private sector organizations have begun to develop training programs and policies aimed at fostering multicultural awareness among managers and employees, instilling a sense of value around cultural diversity and improving the overall management of diversity in the workplace. The key to the success of such programs is breaking down negative stereotypes.

Government managers will need training to understand the "language" and cultural traditions of their employees. They must also be careful not to place value judgments on the culture of workers because such judgments can have a negative effect on productivity and work motivation.

Diversity Means Inclusion, NOT Exclusion.   It has been argued that managers and supervisors must learn and develop a managerial style based on *inclusion* rather than exclusion. For example, it has been traditionally said

TABLE 4.8 Distribution of Population Gains, by Region, Race, and Ethnicity, 1995–2025 (Percentages)

Region	Total	Non-Hispanic White	African American	American Indian	Asian	Latino
U.S.	100.0	21.6	16.5	1.1	16.5	44.3
Northeast	NA[a]	NA[a]	25.2[b]	0.5[b]	39.1[b]	70.1[b]
Midwest	100.0	25.0	25.4	2.7	15.5	31.4
South	100.0	35.2	25.8	0.7	6.1	32.2
West	100.0	18.4	3.1	1.3	22.8	54.4

Notes:
[a] Data not available according to the Census Bureau.
[b] Percentages do not add to 100 because of the declining size of the White population in the Northeast.

Source: U.S. Bureau of the Census, www.census.gov.-

that white men are "members" of a secret, implicit "club," which has greatly enhanced their career opportunities. To address this problem, managers must be trained, at the very least, to include rather than exclude people of color from their frames of reference when they make decisions about training, promotions, and other types of career opportunities.

To go even further, managers and workers must also understand that models of diversity are based on inclusion, not exclusion. Diversity programs do not seek to displace white males but rather to prepare workers and managers to work in a heterogeneous environment in which *everyone* can compete equally for organizational resources. This suggests that training programs should be geared toward the fears of workers, particularly younger employees, about the effects of policies and programs aimed at promoting multiculturalism, pluralism, and diversity. This could ultimately help divert a backlash against diversity programs.

As previously noted, sometimes interracial and interethnic competitions will arise in a workplace where one group believes another is advantaged or has greater employment opportunities. This has been prevalent in the Southwest, where various racial or ethnic groups have pockets of high concentration (see Table 4.8). Again, the challenge for public sector employers is to instill a sense of equality—that inclusion, not exclusion, is the major operating procedure—and all employees have an awareness of it.

Training to Avoid a Backlash Toward Diversity.   Efforts to diversify public and private sector workforces in the 1970s and 1980s were largely a result of legal pressures, which in turn engendered a good deal of resistance and enmity. Indeed, a serious backlash against affirmative action emerged out of the Alan Bakke case in the late 1970s, where Bakke sued the University of California medical school at Davis for "reverse discrimination."[16]

Efforts to promote diversity in the workforce today are impelled or driven not so much by law as economics, which means that at least some employers will be less resistant to diversity. Nonetheless, workers and the general public may continue to resist and oppose diversity measures. Thus government employers in particular are challenged to frame the issue of diversity in a positive and inclusive way that creates an environment in which diversity is truly valued rather than begrudgingly pursued.

Educating Workers on "Who Is Really Qualified for the Job."   Earlier it was noted that public sector employers have been relatively successful in recasting and redeveloping merit exams, at least for entry-level jobs. However, in so doing, they have failed to anticipate the underlying sentiments or resentments of other workers toward those persons of color who are able to pass the newly created merit exams and are subsequently hired or promoted. By now the following scenario will sound all too familiar:

Exams are found to be biased

Employer addresses problem by
reassessing job standards and
requirements and develops a new exam

People of color now able to pass
this new, job-related exam

> Those already in the workforce form
> an impression that the "standards
> have been lowered" and that the persons
> of color who passed this new exam
> are not really qualified for the job
> and that they were hired or promoted
> only because of their race or ethnicity.

These spurious impressions have been a major source of resistance to diversity efforts in the workplace. Managers and workers need to be trained so that these biases can be eradicated; that is, they need to be educated on how people's competencies and qualifications are actually measured. Assuming that people of color are unqualified for their jobs based on culturally biased, non–job related indicators of performance is a problem that calls for serious action if diversity management programs are to succeed.

There are myriad diversity management consultants and several organizations devoted to helping communities and organizations effectively manage diversity. One of the best known, and often used by government employers, is the National Coalition Building Institute (NCBI), a nonprofit leadership training organization that works to eliminate prejudice and intergroup conflict in organizations and communities throughout the world. The NCBI approach is a proactive one, working with organizational "leadership teams" that are taught bridge-building skills to effectively combat intergroup biases and conflicts. Specifically, NCBI teaches participants the many different skills necessary for providing influential leadership in ending discrimination, reducing intergroup conflict, and building multigroup coalitions. Participants learn how to lead, for example, the Prejudice Reduction Workshop, which is made up of a set of activities that help celebrate people's similarities and differences; identify the misinformation they have learned about other groups; identify and heal from internalized oppression; claim pride in their own group identities; learn about the personal impact of discrimination through telling individual stories; and gain empowerment by learning concrete tools for changing bigoted comments and actions. The Prejudice Reduction Workshop has been effectively implemented in hundreds of

TABLE 4.9   Percentage of Legal Immigrants in the U.S. Civilian Labor
Force, Age 16 years and Over, March 1999

	Naturalized Citizen	Not a Citizen
Total	4.5	7.2
Male	4.5	8.4
Female	4.4	5.8

Source: Current Population Survey, March 1999, U.S. Census Bureau,
www.census.gov

schools, universities, public and private organizations, community
groups, churches, and synagogues around the world.

Empowerment Strategies

Empowerment in a very broad sense has assumed a host of meanings.
For purposes here, it is a process through which people of color will come
to share power alongside other groups and partake as equal partners in
decisionmaking. In short, it refers to increasing the institutional power of
people of color or maximizing their participation in organizational policy and decisionmaking.

In a practical sense, governments can promote empowerment by
breaking down some of the institutional barriers to it. Some of these
issues were addressed earlier. For example, institutional barriers to
empowerment include negative social attitudes toward African
Americans, Latinos, Asians, and American Indians. Bureaucratic deci-
sional and policy processes, which tend to be closed off to people of color,
also pose constraints. By combating these barriers, people of color will
acquire the power and right to participate in the political, social, and economic planning and governance of this nation. Ultimately, resource distribution will be more equitable across the board.

Issues Surrounding Immigrants

As noted in Chapter 1, there has been a major influx of immigrants into
the United States over the past decade or so, and this trend is likely to
increase in the next several decades. Moreover, employment analysts estimate that as of 1999, about a third of the 15.7 million immigrants in this

country had entered it illegally. Overall, immigrants are said to compose 12 percent of the nation's workers. Table 4.9 presents data on the percentages of legal immigrants in the U.S. labor force.[17] Obviously, it is impossible to get a complete or accurate reflection of immigrants in the workforce or labor force, since data are not available for illegal immigrants.

Immigrants, whether here legally or illegally, tend to work predominately in the private sector, and, according to the U.S. Bureau of Labor Statistics, are heavily concentrated in such low-paying, arduous jobs as meat packers, poultry plant workers, gardeners, hotel maids, seamstresses (sometimes in sweatshops), restaurant workers, and produce pickers. Seasonal workers here legally, recently dubbed "guest workers," come mostly from Mexico and tend to work on farms, from North Carolina to Georgia, Arkansas to Idaho.[18] Illegal immigrants who hire themselves out on a daily basis work all sorts of odd jobs, from yard work to construction. For example, the *esquineros*, or men of the corner, gather each morning on designated street corners in cities all over the country, where they are picked up by the truckload for various daily jobs and are paid up to $100 a day or more, depending on the type of work. Whether they are here legally or illegally, immigrants are a major part of the U.S. labor force.[19]

Immigrants who are here legally and are trained professionals can be found in private or public sector jobs in medicine, engineering, computer technology, and the like. An increasing number of immigrants are arriving from Eastern European countries, in addition to Asian countries. Interestingly, the U.S. Congress in October 2000 passed a bill that increases significantly the number of visas available for educated foreign-born persons in order to temporarily fill highly specialized jobs in the United States, especially in the computer and technology industry. The measure was spurred by the great demand for jobs in high-tech industries and low supply of American labor with the requisite skills.[20] Of course, this raises questions around why the United States is not investing more to prepare its citizens for these highly specialized jobs or why public and private organizations are not training existing workers to fill them.

The challenge for employers is to ensure that immigrants or foreign-born workers are successfully integrated into the workplace. Some of the problems discussed earlier are relevant, for example, training to dispel potential negative stereotypes about Asians, Hispanics, or Eastern Europeans; taking steps to rid the workplace of any harassment that might be directed toward immigrant workers; and ensuring that incumbent workers do not have misperceptions about organizational job opportunities, such as, immigrants are taking jobs away from American-born workers. It should be noted, however, that American labor unions argue that organizations, by recruiting and hiring foreign-born workers, sometimes displace American workers and depress pay.[21] These are potential challenges that government employers may need to address to the extent that immigrants are part of their workforces.

Conclusion

Government employers face many challenges vis-à-vis developing diversity programs as they pertain to people of color. Employers will certainly need to tailor the programs so that they are appropriate and relevant to the different racial and ethnic groups composing their workforce. As we will see in subsequent chapters, although there are many similarities in areas that need to be targeted (e.g., training), the actual content of diversity programs and strategies depends on the primary dimension of diversity being addressed. The following chapter looks at diversity issues as they pertain to women in government workforces.

Notes

1. Sana Siwolop, "Nooses, Symbols of Race Hatred, at Center of Workplace Lawsuits," *New York Times,* July 10, 2000, pp. A1, A16.

2. See, for example, J. Edward Kellough, "Affirmative Action and Equal Employment Opportunity," *Review of Public Personnel Administration,* Fall 1997. Symposium.

3. See, for example, Norma M. Riccucci, "Merit, Equity, and Test Validity: A New Look at an Old Problem," *Administration and Society,* May 1991, pp. 74–93.

4. The "rule of three," another plum of civil service systems, has also impeded entry-level hiring of people of color.

5. The case law where people of color file suit against a government employer for discriminatory promotion exams is abundant, particularly in the area of promotional exams in police and fire departments. For a typical case, see *Bryant v. City of Chicago* (2000).

6. It is not uncommon for people of color to be denied, or perceive they are being denied, opportunities to gain the job experience necessary for promotions. See, for example, *Reynolds v. Roberts* (2000).

7. See www.mspb.gov.

8. See Sana Siwolop, "When Your Boss Keeps Raising the Bar," *New York Times,* December 6, 2000, p. G1.

9. See Siwolop, "When Your Boss," p. A1.

10. *Torres v. Pisano and New York University* (1997) at 628.

11. *Schwapp v. Town of Avon* (1997) at 108.

12. *Richardson v. New York State Dept. of Correctional Service* (1999).

13. *Robinson v. City and County of Denver*, 2000 WL 1159061 (Colo. App. 2000).

14. *Workforce 2020* (Indianapolis: Hudson Institute, 1997), p. 115.

15. Ibid., p. 9.

16. *Regents v. Bakke* (1978).

17. For federal employment, under Executive Order 11935, only U.S. citizens and nationals (residents of American Samoa and Swains Island) may compete for competitive jobs. Agencies are permitted to hire noncitizens only when there are no qualified citizens available. A noncitizen hired in the absence of qualified citizens may only be given an excepted appointment and does not acquire competitive civil service status. He or she may not be promoted or reassigned to another position in the competitive service, except in situations where a qualified citizen is not available. The noncitizen may be hired only if permitted by the appropriations act and the immigration law (see http://www.usajobs.opm.gov/b1m.htm).

18. See Ginger Thompson and Steven Greenhouse, "Mexican 'Guest Workers': A Project Worth a Try?" *New York Times*, April 3, 2001, p. A4.

19. See, for example, Charlie LeDuff, "For Migrants, Hard Work in Hostile Suburbs," *New York Times*, September 24, 2000, pp. 1, 42.

20. Lizette Alvarez, "Congress Backs Big Increase in Visas for Skilled Workers," *New York Times*, October 4, 2000, pp. A1, A24.

21. See, for example, Alvarez, "Congress Backs Big Increase."

Additional Reading

Alvarez, Lizette. "Congress Backs Big Increase in Visas for Skilled Workers." *New York Times*, October 4, 2000, pp. A1, A24.

Best Practices in Achieving Workforce Diversity. Washington, D.C.: U.S. Department of Commerce and the National Partnership for Reinventing Government Benchmarking Study, October 2000.

Carnevale, Anthony P., and Susan C. Stone. *The American Mosaic: An In-Depth Report on the Future of Diversity at Work*. New York: McGraw-Hill, 1995.

Copeland, Lennie. "Valuing Diversity, Part 2: Pioneers and Champions of Change." *Personnel*, July 1988, pp. 44–49.

Goldstein, Irwin L., and Patrice Gilliam. "Training System Issues in the Year 2000." *American Psychologist* 45 (1990): 134–143.

Henderson, George. *Cultural Diversity in the Workplace*. Westport, Conn.: Quorum, 1994.

John, Martha Tyler, and Donald G. Roberts. *Cultural Adaptation in the Workplace*. New York: Garland, 1996.

Loden, Marilyn. *Implementing Diversity*. Chicago: Irwin Professional, 1996.

Lynch, Frederick R. *The Diversity Machine*. New York: Free Press, 1997.

Ospina, Sonia M. *Illusions of Opportunity: Employee Expectations and Workplace Inequality.* Ithaca, N.Y.: Cornell University Press, 1996.

Panzarella, Robert. "The Impact of Tutoring Minority Recruits for Civil Service Exams for Police Officer Selection." *Review of Public Personnel Administration*, Spring 1986, pp. 59–71.

Rice, Mitchell F., ed. *Diversity and Public Organizations.* Dubuque: Kendall/Hunt, 1996.

Tayeb, Monir H. *The Management of a Multicultural Workforce.* New York: Wiley, 1996.

Tsui, Anne S., and Barbara A. Gutek. *Demographic Differences in Organizations: Current Research and Future Directions.* Lanham, Md.: Lexington, 1999.

Wilson, Elisabeth M., and Paul A. Iles. "Managing Diversity: An Employment and Service Delivery Challenge." *International Journal of Public Sector Management* 12 (1999): 27–48.

Cases

Bryant v. City of Chicago, 200 F.3d 1092 (7th Cir. 2000).

Regents of the University of California v. Bakke, 438 U.S. 265 (1978).

Reynolds v. Roberts, 202 F.3d 1303 (11th Cir. 2000).

Richardson v. New York State Dept. of Correctional Service, 180 F.3d 426 (2d Cir. 1999).

Robinson v. City and County of Denver, 2000 WL 1159061 (Colo. App. 2000).

Schwapp v. Town of Avon, 118 F.2d 106 (2d Cir. 1997).

Torres v. Pisano and New York University, 116 F.3d 625 (2d Cir. 1997).

5

Diversity Management and Women in Public Sector Workforces

Women have constituted a significant share of public sector jobs and, as the demographers have forecasted, they will continue to do so in the coming decades. As we saw in Chapter 1, women of all races account for the greatest gains in employment by the year 2008. Although women have made some gains in government jobs, gender differences in the workplace, just like racial and ethnic diversity, have resulted in a host of discriminatory practices and biases against women, which ultimately hinder the overall effectiveness and productivity of government organizations. A recent report by *Advancing Women*, a women's business Web site that provides wide-ranging online support for women business owners, stated that "sexism at work and child rearing duties at home are proving to be the most intractable barriers for women in the workplace perhaps because they are not as susceptible to legal challenges."[1]

As women continue to increase their share of public sector jobs, governments at every level must be prepared to develop programs and policies that not only eradicate discriminatory practices but also work to attract and retain this important and considerable cohort of workers.

This chapter begins by taking a brief look at the gender mix in public workforces at the federal, state, and local levels of government. It then examines strategies that government employers have advanced or could develop to effectively manage the workplace so that it is a more congenial setting for women and accommodating of their needs and interests. As noted previously, a more content, satisfied workforce may be the key to greater productivity and improved governance.

TABLE 5.1   Federal Executive Branch (Nonpostal) Employment, by Gender, 1986–1998

	1986	1988	1990	1992	1996	1998
Total	2,083,985	2,125,148	2,150,359	2,175,715	1,890,406	1,804,591
Gender						
Women	861,182	897,099	927,104	945,546	831,840	801,250
% Women	41.3	42.2	43.1	43.5	44.0	44.4
Men	1,222,803	1,228,049	1,223,255	1,230,169	1,058,566	1,003,341
% Men	58.7	57.8	56.9	56.5	56.0	55.6

Source: U.S. Office of Personnel Management (OPM), www.opm.gov

Women in Public Sector Employment

Tables 5.1 and 5.2 provide a snapshot of women in federal, state, and local government jobs. As the data show, women's employment in public sector jobs has steadily increased since the mid-1980s, particularly for women of color.

The research further shows that women tend to be concentrated in lower-level, lower-paying positions in public sector workforces (see Tables 5.3, 5.4). As the tables show, the higher-level professional jobs, which carry greater levels of authority and pay, are dominated by men, while the lower-level jobs are filled by women, in particular women of color.

Similar to the patterns for people of color, as discussed in Chapter 4, the research also shows that women tend to be concentrated in occupations or agencies that have traditionally employed them (see tables 5.5, 5.6). Table 5.6, for example, illustrates the relatively low concentrations of women in such professions or occupations as police, firefighting, corrections, and sanitation (addressed in greater detail later in this chapter).

As we saw with the data on people of color in Chapter 4, several important pieces of information can be gleaned from the employment patterns of women in government workforces. First, women continue to be segregated into departments or jobs traditionally associated with "women's work." Government employers will need to ensure that women have equal opportunities to access any and all occupations for which they qualify. This is a matter of fairness, equity, and choice (i.e., it's

TABLE 5.2   State and Local Government Employment, by Gender, Race, and Ethnicity, 1985–1997 (Percentages)

	Women		
	1985	1989	1997
Total	1,952,334	2,227,265	2,307,015
Race/Ethnicity			
Non minority	29.5	29.6	29.6
Total minority female	11.6	12.3	14.8
African American	8.7	9.3	10.0
Latino	2.0	2.0	3.3
Asian/Pacific Islander	0.7	0.9	1.2
American Indian/ Alaska Native	0.2	0.1	0.3
	Men		
	1985	1989	1997
Total	2,789,174	3,030,166	2,897,947
Race/Ethnicity			
Non minority	73.6	72.4	70.6
Total minority male	13.2	13.8	14.6
African American	8.9	9.0	8.7
Latino	3.2	3.5	4.2
Asian/Pacific Islander	0.8	1.0	1.3
American Indian/ Alaska Native	0.3	0.3	0.4

not a matter of questioning why a woman would want to be, for example, a garbage collector, but that women have the *choice* to enter this occupation if they so desire).

Another important point to garner by the data is that women continue to be concentrated in lower-level, lower-paying jobs. To the extent that employers are serious about managing diversity, they will need to develop programs and policies aimed at enhancing the promotion opportunities for women in the workplace.

TABLE 5.3 Federal Employment Trends by White-Collar Occupational Category (Women Only), 1986–1998

		Total		Non minority		Minority		Black		Hispanic		Asian/Pacific Islander		American Indian/ Alaska Native	
		#	%	#	%	#	%	#	%	#	%	#	%	#	%
Professional	1986	112,887	100.0	87,770	77.8	25,117	22.2	13,417	11.9	3,760	3.3	6,101	5.4	1,839	1.6
	1996	172,315	100.0	126,978	73.7	45,337	26.3	22,095	12.8	7,628	4.4	12,467	7.2	3,147	1.8
	1998	171,064	100.0	124,635	72.9	46,429	27.1	22,213	13.0	7,796	4.6	13,035	7.6	3,385	2.0
Administrative	1986	166,819	100.0	123,608	74.1	13,211	25.9	31,323	18.7	6,584	3.9	3,348	2.0	2,046	1.2
	1996	220,664	100.0	154,270	69.9	66,394	30.1	44,230	20.0	12,340	5.6	6,463	2.9	3,361	1.5
	1998	225,649	100.0	155,144	68.8	70,505	31.2	46,933	20.8	13,066	5.8	6,920	3.1	3,586	1.6
Technical	1986	178,684	100.0	117,914	66.0	60,770	34.0	44,018	24.6	7,284	4.1	3,783	2.1	5,685	3.2
	1996	218,475	100.0	131,134	60.0	87,341	40.0	60,194	27.6	13,022	6.0	7,267	3.3	6,858	3.1
	1998	210,409	100.0	123,799	58.8	86,610	41.2	58,645	27.9	13,649	6.5	7,443	3.5	6,873	3.3
Clerical	1986	354,567	100.0	231,639	65.3	122,928	34.7	89,491	25.2	18,962	5.3	8,377	2.4	6,098	1.7
	1996	185,948	100.0	107,431	57.8	78,517	42.2	54,556	29.3	12,634	6.8	6,399	3.4	4,928	2.7
	1998	162,669	100.0	92,509	56.9	70,160	43.1	47,867	29.4	11,632	7.2	6,052	3.7	4,609	2.8
Other	1986	3,296	100.0	1,987	60.3	1,309	39.7	909	27.6	230	7.0	105	3.2	65	2.0
	1996	5,751	100.0	3,114	54.1	2,637	45.9	1,723	30.0	577	10.0	194	3.4	143	2.5
	1998	5,784	100.0	3,031	52.4	2,753	47.6	1,747	30.2	681	11.8	186	3.2	139	2.4
Total White-Collar[a]	1986	816,253	100.0	562,918	69.0	253,335	31.0	179,068	21.9	36,820	4.5	21,714	2.7	15,733	1.9
	1996	803,153	100.0	522,927	65.1	280,226	34.9	182,798	22.8	46,201	5.8	32,790	4.1	18,437	2.3
	1998	775,575	100.0	499,118	64.4	276,457	35.6	177,405	22.9	46,824	6.0	33,636	4.3	18,592	2.4

Note: [a]The total white-collar totals shown for 1986 do not include unspecified counts.
Source: U.S. Office of Personnel Management, Central Personnel Data File (CPDF).

65

TABLE 5.4 Employment of Women by Occupation in State and Local Governments, 1985,[a] 1989,[b] 1997[c]

| | | | Women | | | | | |
	Year	Total Employment	Total Women %	White %	African American %	Latira %	Asian %	Native American %
Total (all occupations)	1985	1,952,334	41.2	29.5	8.7	2.0	0.7	0.2
	1989	2,227,265	42.4	29.6	9.3	2.0	0.9	0.1
	1997	2,307,015	44.4	29.6	10.0	3.3	1.2	0.3
Officials/ Administrators	1985	70,602	28.0	22.9	3.9	0.8	0.3	0.1
	1989	89,727	30.7	24.1	24.	4.9	1.1	0.1
	1997	99,124	33.4	26.3	4.9	1.5	0.6	0
Professionals	1985	447,784	46.9	36.3	7.2	1.6	1.6	0.2
	1989	566,131	49.3	37.2	8.2	1.9	1.8	0.2
	1997	685,873	53.1	38.1	9.4	3.0	2.3	0.3
Technicians	1985	186,276	39.5	28.5	8.2	1.8	0.8	0.2
	1989	198,820	40.0	27.8	8.6	2.4	1.1	0.2
	1997	190,913	41.8	28.1	8.7	3.4	1.5	0.2
Protective Service	1985	68,852	9.5	6.4	2.6	0.5	0	0.1
	1989	104,204	12.3	7.8	3.6	0.7	0.1	0.1
	1997	155,909	16.1	9.3	5.3	1.2	0.1	0.1
Paraprofessionals	1985	259,808	70.6	44.0	22.7	2.9	0.6	0.3
	1989	276,867	71.9	44.2	22.9	3.5	0.8	0.4
	1997	269,145	73.0	43.5	22.6	5.2	1.3	0.4
Office/Clerical	1985	767,246	37.8	64.7	15.9	5.4	1.3	0.4
	1989	834,938	37.5	62.4	16.9	6.1	1.6	0.4
	1997	765,193	36.8	58.4	17.8	8.0	2.0	0.5

TABLE 5.4 . (continued)

| | Year | Total Employment | Women | | | | | |
			Total Women %	White %	African American %	Latina %	Asian %	Native American %
Skilled/craft	1985	14,636	3.7	2.7	0.7	0.1	0	0
	1989	17,264	3.9	2.8	0.8	0.2	0	0
	1997	20,940	5.2	3.6	17.8	0.3	0.1	0
Service/maintenance	1985	137,130	19.6	10.6	7.5	1.1	0.2	0.1
	1989	139,294	20.2	10.7	7.8	1.3	0.3	0.1
	1997	119,918	22.4	11.3	8.8	1.7	0.4	0.2

Notes:

[a] Calculated from unpublished EEOC report.

[b] U.S. Equal Employment Opportunity Commission. *Job Patterns for Minorities and Women in State and Local Governments, 1989.* Washington, D.C., 1990.

[c] U.S. Equal Employment Opportunity Commission. *Job Patterns for Minorities and Women in State and Local Governments, 1997.* Washington, D.C., 1998.

TABLE 5.5 Distribution of Employees in Federal Government, by Gender, Race, Ethnicity, and Agency, 1998 (Percentages, Women Only)

Agency	Total Women of Color	African American	Latina	Asian or Pacific Islander	American Indian or Alaska Native	Whites
Total Executive Branch	16.1	10.3	2.7	1.9	1.1	28.4
Agriculture	10.8	6.8	2.1	0.9	1.0	31.3
Commerce	16.7	12.7	1.8	1.8	0.3	31.1
Defense	12.1	7.5	2.2	2.0	0.4	25.7
Energy	12.1	8.0	2.5	1.1	0.5	25.8
Health & Human Services	28.7	12.0	1.6	2.5	12.5	31.1
Housing & Urban Development	31.9	25.6	4.0	1.7	0.7	27.4
Interior	12.6	2.7	1.8	0.8	7.4	25.7
Justice	14.9	9.6	3.8	1.2	0.3	23.9
Labor	23.4	18.1	3.3	1.6	0.4	26.4
State	14.8	10.5	2.0	2.1	0.2	31.1
Transportation	8.5	6.0	1.3	0.8	0.4	19.0
Treasury	22.8	16.1	4.6	1.7	0.5	32.5
Veterans Affairs	20.0	13.3	2.8	3.5	0.4	34.5
Total	44.4[a]					

Note: [a]Percentage of all women, all races, in executive branch of government.
Source: U.S. Office of Personnel Management (OPM), www.opm.gov.

TABLE 5.6   Percentage of Women in Selected State and Local Government
Professions, 1985–1997

		Percentage Women	
	1985	1995	1997
Firefighting	0.9	6.3	7.5
Police	9.2	26.8	27.7
Corrections	15.4	33.7	34.5
Sanitation	2.4	13.6	15.1

Sources: "State and Local Government Information, Summary Report for 1985
EEO-4 Survey" (Washington, D.C.: Equal Employment Opportunity
Commission), 1985; *Job Patterns for Minorities and Women in State and
Local Government*, 1995 (Washington, D.C.: EEOC, 1995) and *Job Patterns for
Minorities and Women in State and Local Government*, 1997 (Washington,
D.C.: EEOC, 1998).

Strategies for Managing Diversity around Gender

In developing strategies to accommodate women's needs and interests in
the workplace, it is important for employers to recognize that race makes a
difference. For example, the employment histories of white women differs
from that of African American or Latina women. Chapter 3 discussed
diversity strategies for people of color and provides insights around diversity programs that are relevant for women of color. But outlining strategies
for each racial and ethnic group of women is not the purpose of this chapter, which addresses diversity issues pertaining to women in general.

Opportunities for the Promotion and Advancement of Women

By now, we are all familiar with the problem known as the "glass ceiling." This concept refers to the artificial barriers that keep women from
reaching upper-level management positions in public and private sector
organizations.[2] A number of studies conducted by researchers as well as
government agencies (e.g., the U.S. Department of Labor[3] and the U.S.
Merit System Protection Board[4]) have consistently found that there is, in
fact, a glass ceiling that prevents women from advancing to upper-level
management positions.

These studies also identify the various institutional barriers that create the glass ceilings:

- Recruitment practices involving reliance on word-of-mouth and employee referral networking; the use of executive search and referral firms in which affirmative action/EEO requirements were not always made known.
- Developmental practices and credential-building experiences, including advanced education and career-enhancing assignments (e.g., to corporate committees and task forces and special projects)—which are traditional precursors to advancement—were often not available to minorities and women.
- Subtle assumptions, attitudes, and stereotypes that affect how managers sometimes view women's potential for advancement and, in some cases, their effectiveness on the job.
- Promotion practices that keep women out of the critical grades at the federal level of employment, GS 9 and GS 11, which are the pipelines through which people must pass in moving upward to higher-level jobs.
- Perceptions by managers that women are less committed to their jobs than men, particularly those women who are in the first five years of their career.
- Women with families are sometimes perceived as less dedicated to their jobs.
- Women are often held to higher standards of excellence or moral conduct than men.
- Accountability for Equal Employment Opportunity responsibilities did not reach to senior level executives and corporate decisionmakers.[5]

The U.S. Merit System Protection Board (MSPB) study of the glass ceiling in the federal government workforce found that women do confront inequitable barriers to career advancement; women of color face "a double disadvantage." The study revealed that, on average, women of color are promoted less often than white women with the same qualifications.

Surveys conducted at the state and local levels of government also reveal the existence of a glass ceiling. For example, one survey found the following:

- States have a poorer track record than local governments on women acquiring a proportionate share of top jobs.
- Racial and ethnic minority women trail behind white women in access to top government jobs.
- Few women hold high-level political appointments to cabinet positions:

    At the county level, women made up 18.6 percent of the chief appointed administrative officers, and 31.8 percent of other top appointed officials.

    In municipalities, which include towns and villages as well as cities, women were 12.5 percent of chief appointed administrative officers and 26.2 percent of other key appointments in 1990.

    Over 95 percent of the top female appointees in county and municipal governments were white.
- Women hold the greatest proportion of top jobs in county government. Women are a higher proportion of officials and administrators in counties (39.7 percent) than they are in states. But the rest of the county workforce also employs more women (53.2 percent), probably because more county employees are engaged in the traditionally female areas of health and public welfare.
- Women hold fewer top city managerial jobs, but their representation more closely reflects women's share of the city workforce. Women are only 26.2 percent of city officials and administrators, but they are nearly proportionately represented compared with their presence in the rest of the city workforce (27.8 percent). City services in traditionally male areas, such as highways, safety, and parks, may explain women's low overall participation rate.[6]

The Civil Rights Act of 1991 called for the establishment of a Glass Ceiling Commission to study artificial barriers to the advancement of women and persons of color in the workplace and to make recommendations for overcoming such barriers. In addition, the act established the Frances Perkins–Elizabeth Hanford Dole National Award for Diversity and Excellence in American Executive Management to be presented annually to organizations that make substantial strides in promoting women and persons of color to management and decisionmaking positions. Notwithstanding, the glass ceiling persists. Indeed, former Secretary of Labor Alexis M. Herman recently stated that "a double-pane glass ceiling impedes women" in the workplace. Not only are women facing barriers to career advancement, Herman states, but those women who "squeeze through that crack [into senior management positions] have yet to break the second pane—the barrier of disparate pay. We find that female executives routinely earn less than their male counterparts."[7]

It is axiomatic that government workforces will need to address the glass ceiling problem so that women can ascend to the middle and upper professional and policymaking positions within public sector organizations. This may in turn increase the relevance and hence effectiveness of the programs and policies aimed at accommodating diversity within organizations. In fact, some research has shown that gender as well as racial diversity in the upper levels of organizations leads to more progressive policies aimed at gender and racial diversity within organizations.[8] In other words, the success of diversity programs within the workforce may hinge on the representation of women and persons of color in upper-level positions.[9]

One approach to moving women and persons of color into upper level positions is through management/professional development programs. For example, such programs may be aimed at preparing, over the course of two to four years, secretaries and clerical workers—predominately female occupations—for management positions. The programs could operate in any number of ways, including apprenticeship training programs that offer formal course work to complement on-the-job training under an incumbent manager.

As the MSPB points out, experience and education are two of the most critical factors for career advancement in the federal government. Creating opportunities to improve women's experience in certain jobs or job functions to increase their formal education could help break down barriers to career advancement. Some government employers, in conjunction with employee unions, have instituted programs to help government workers pay for courses at local colleges and universities. Providing flextime, enabling workers to have some control over their own work schedules, further ensures that they can attend classes without jeopardizing their jobs.

Government employers are encouraged to alleviate some of the problems directly attributed to the glass ceiling. For example, employers could be more vigilant about how information around promotional opportunities is disseminated. In other words, employers can address the problem of information networks that keep women kept out of the "loop" in terms of promotions and other professional opportunities. Developing formal mentoring programs that partner senior workers with women seeking advancement can also be beneficial. Ensuring that women have access to the "pipeline" jobs that are prerequisites to higher-level positions is essential. Training, which will be addressed in further detail later in this chapter, would also help those managers who have negative assumptions about women's potential for career advancement.

Other concerns and questions employers can resolve include:

- Is there an informal "bonding" between men that has a negative impact on women?
- Are women more likely than men to be directed into staff rather than line positions by their mentors, and does this make them less competitive than men for promotions?
- Are there informal policies in federal agencies that have the effect of slowing women's opportunities for advancement?

Creating Opportunities for Women in Nontraditional Jobs. In addition to the glass ceiling, the problem of glass or "sticky walls" has also hurt women's career opportunities. Glass walls refer to barriers that perpetuate occupational segregation or keep women in certain jobs and professions and out of others (see Tables 5.5, 5.6).

Diversity must ensure equal access for women not only within job categories but across occupations as well. As employers strive to diversify all job levels in their organizations, governments must also work to diversify traditionally male occupations. Professions in state and local government that have historically kept women out include firefighting, police, corrections—collectively referred to as the uniformed services—and sanitation (see Table 5.6). Although women have certainly made significant progress over the years, especially in corrections, resistance continues to the integration of women in these professions. Firefighting in particular resists hiring women or even appointing women to uniformed service in voluntary fire departments.

One intractable barrier to women's employment in police, firefighting, corrections, and sanitation has been the physical agility exams for such jobs. Although no one would dispute the fact that physical strength is a requirement for these jobs, the amount of physical strength required for each particular job has often come into question. For example, it has been argued that the job of a police officer is much more sedentary than that of a firefighter, which has implications for the actual strength requirements of the job.

The real issue behind physical agility requirements rests in whether the civil service exams for physical strength are job related. A surfeit of lawsuits in the 1980s uncovered gross disparities in the exams.[10] In some cases, police, fire, corrections, and sanitation departments relied on outdated or outmoded tests—which had nothing to do with the job. Squeezing a hand dynamometer or performing a certain number of chinups, which are tasks that would never be required of a firefighter, were routinely included in agility exams.

When courts examine whether physical agility exams are job related, they are inquiring about the *validity* of the exams—the degree to which the exams measure the skills associated with the job. Interestingly, when some cities were forced to develop new agility exams, they relied on what is known as "concurrent validity,"[11] where job incumbents are tested in order to develop performance measures for the job. In other words, persons already on the job (in this case men) were setting the standards for necessary job performance; job candidates were then tested against these new standards. In effect, women seeking positions in the uniformed services were not necessarily being tested for the actual strength requirements of the jobs, but whether they possessed the same amount of strength that men already on the job possessed.[12] Overall, women were unable to pass these new exams.

However, many cities relied on other methods for validating their exams. Once these exams were made more job related, women were able to pass the new agility tests. Nonetheless, women began to face other barriers in the uniformed services: Local governments made no provisions for the resistance that women invariably faced once hired into traditionally male jobs. Incumbent male workers in many cases, particularly in fire departments, were unwilling to accept their female counterparts. Another round of lawsuits ensued,[13] in which women were found to be habitually sexually harassed and ostracized by men on the job. While some of these problems have been alleviated, women continue to face barriers in uniformed service jobs, most notably, acceptance by male counterparts. The continued existence of these problems impedes workplace harmony and can only lead to disruptions in organizational performance and productivity.

The Mommy Track.   About ten years ago, an "expert" on career women, Felice Schwartz, wrote an article published in the *Harvard Business Review*,[14] arguing that women managers are different from their male counterparts in that women tend to eventually leave work to have children, thereby cutting back on their work or professional commitments. In effect, according to Schwartz, organizations pay a high price here because they don't get a full return on their investments in women (e.g., in the form of training for higher-level jobs). To address this problem, Schwartz advocated an organizational policy that would bifurcate the career path for women. One path would be "career primary," for women who set work as their primary goal. These are women who (high-level executives believe) would not leave their career to raise a family. The other path, dubbed the "mommy track," would be for "career and family" women. They are not considered to be as serious about their careers and, in effect, would not be groomed for senior-level positions. Rather, they would be tracked or steered into a dead-end career path.

Although the mommy track may not be formally discussed in organizations, it is obviously a strategy that could reinforce organizational and social prejudice against women. It is a step backward in terms of the progress women are making in the workplace, and it penalizes women for a decision to have children. Yet men who have made it to the upper echelons of organizations have done so by relying on their spouses to raise the children and maintain the home. In essence, the mommy track works against every credo that has been advanced around managing a diverse workforce. Indeed, as will be discussed shortly, organizations working to stay on the fast, productive track seem to be making provisions for women to balance work and family needs as an incentive to recruit and retain high-quality working women.

Eradicating Sexual Harassment

Sexual harassment continues to be a pernicious problem in the workplace. National attention centered on it in 1991, during the confirmation hearings of Clarence Thomas to become a justice on the U.S. Supreme Court. University of Oklahoma law professor Anita Hill alleged that Thomas sexually harassed her while he was director of the U.S. Equal Employment Opportunity Commission (EEOC), and she was a staff member there. Thomas barely won confirmation—by a Senate vote of 52 to 48—to the High Court. Notwithstanding, the Hill-Thomas hearings brought new ferment to the problem of sexual harassment in the work-place.

Not long after the Hill-Thomas debacle, the federal government was inundated by sexual harassment claims. In fact, in 1994, Paula Corbin Jones filed suit against President Bill Clinton, alleging that he sexually harassed her while she was a state worker and he was governor of Arkansas. The national attention drawn to the president's sexual procliv-ities ultimately led to the Monica Lewinsky scandal. Lewinsky, a twenty-one-year-old intern at the White House, was alleged to have had a con-sensual sexual relationship with President Clinton. Although not a sexual harassment case, the affair galvanized the nation's attention around appropriate sexual or romantic behavior in the workplace.

Sexual harassment is illegal in public and private sector employment under a number of statutes. Most important for noncriminal sexual harassment is Title VII of the Civil Rights Act of 1964 as amended by the Equal Employment Opportunity Act of 1972. The EEOC, in its 1980 "Guidelines on Discrimination Because of Sex," took the position that sexual harassment is a form of gender discrimination.

The definition of sexual harassment continues to expand as courts con-tinue to define more types of behavior as sexual harassment. Behaviors that are proscribed by statutory and common law include the following:

- Unwanted, uninvited pressure for sexual favors
- Unwanted, uninvited pressure for dates
- Unwanted, uninvited letters, telephone calls, or materials of a sexual nature
- Unwanted, uninvited touching, leaning over, cornering, or pinching
- Unwanted, uninvited sexually suggestive looks or gestures
- Unwanted, uninvited sexual teasing, jokes, remarks, or ques-tions[15]

Sexual harassment continues to be widespread in the federal govern-ment, as a 1995 study conducted by the Merit Systems Protection Board (MSPB) found. The report stated that "in 1994, 44 percent of women and 19 percent of men responding to [the MSPB] survey reported that they had experienced some form of unwanted sexual attention during the pre-ceding 2 years."[16] The study also found that "coworkers and other employees, rather than individuals in the supervisory chain, continue to be the primary source of sexual harassment in the Federal workplace." The report concluded that "sexual harassment cost the Federal Government an estimated $327 million during the 2-year period April 1992 to April 1994." This amount includes the cost of sick leave, job turnover, and productivity losses as a result of sexual harassment.

In 1986, the U.S. Supreme Court issued a landmark ruling that made sexual harassment a prohibited form of gender discrimination. In *Meritor Savings Bank v. Vinson*, the Court ruled that "a violation of Title VII may be predicated on either of two types of sexual harassment: harassment that involves the conditioning of concrete employment benefits on sexual favors, and harassment that, while not affecting economic benefits, creates a *hostile* or offensive working environment."[17] In the first type of sexual harassment, known as "quid pro quo" sexual harassment, the plaintiff attempts to prove that job benefits, such as a pay increase or promotion, were denied because sexual favors were not granted to the harasser.

The second type of sexual harassment involves the hostile environment standard; this is important because it suggests that a violation of Title VII on a sexual harassment claim is not dependent on the victim's loss of promotion or employment. Ultimately, the Court's ruling encourages employers to develop policies and complaint procedures that will protect employees from unwanted, unwelcome sexual advances.

In 1993, the U.S. Supreme Court issued another ruling in *Harris v. Forklift Systems, Inc.*, that further refined the standards for determining harassing conditions. In a unanimous ruling, the *Harris* Court said that "Whether an environment is 'hostile' or 'abusive' can be determined only by looking at all the circumstances. These may include the frequency of the discriminatory conduct; its severity; whether it is physically threatening or humiliating, or a mere offensive utterance; and whether it unreasonably interferes with an employees' work performance."[18] This decision is important for a number of reasons; for instance, it held that psychological harm need not be demonstrated by a woman alleging hostile environment. Justice Sandra Day O'Connor, who wrote the opinion, stated that you don't need to have a nervous breakdown before Title VII will protect you from sexual harassment.

In 1998, the U.S. Supreme Court widened workplace sexual harassment claims, ruling that Title VII also protects employees from same-sex harassment. The unanimous decision in *Oncale v. Sundowner Offshore*

Services[19] extended the law beyond male-female sexual harassment to cover people of the same sex. The Court ruled that it was the conduct itself, and not the sex or motivation of the people involved, that determined whether sexual harassment amounted to discrimination because of sex. Sexual desire, whether heterosexual or homosexual, the Court said, is not a necessary element of such a case (the *Oncale* case will be discussed in greater detail in Chapter 8).

Also in 1998, the U.S. Supreme Court issued two other rulings that will greatly affect employer liability in sexual harassment suits. In *Faragher v. City of Boca Raton*[20] and *Burlington Industries v. Ellerth*,[21] the High Court, in 7–2 votes (Justices Clarence Thomas and Antonin Scalia dissented from the majority), ruled that an employer is liable under Title VII for its supervisors' sexual harassment, even if it did not know about the misconduct. The Court further ruled that in some cases, an employer can defend itself by showing that it took reasonable steps to prevent harassment on the job.

It is very common for government employers to have policies on sexual harassment. Enforcement, however, is key to not only eradicating the problem and its concomitant high costs but to avoiding lawsuits as well. Ensuring that the workplace is free from harassing behaviors of a sexual nature would seem to constitute, therefore, a high priority for government employers.

Developing Family-Friendly Benefits and Policies

Employee benefits are extremely important to both public and private sector employees. And for workers with dependents, benefit packages may be vital. Family leave, day care, and flexible schedules are among the benefits that have provided some sense of security to workers and their families. Today, employee benefits account for as much as 40 percent of the total cost of employee compensation; with the growing complexity of family concerns and needs, this is expected to increase by the next century.

Although family-friendly benefits are not intended solely for women, it is generally women's needs and interests that tend to be served by them. Women are the ones who bear children and will inevitably need a period of leave for childbirth. In addition, women tend be the primary caregivers for children and/or elderly parents or grandparents. It has been estimated that close to 75 percent of caregivers in our society are women.[22]

Nevertheless, women are remaining in the workforce at greater than twice the rate they did in 1960 after having children, and about 56 percent return to work within a year of giving birth. Working moms are also putting in more hours than they did in the past, their work hours increasing by 129 percent between 1969 and 1996. The bottom line is that there has been an increasing number of working moms in the past few decades because women want to work.

Because some workers may feel slighted by "family-benefit" programs (e.g., they have no children; the organizations limit "family" to married, heterosexual couples, etc.), some public employers, to ensure fairness and equity, have instituted cafeteria-style benefit programs, which allow all employees to select benefits from an array or menu of choices to best meet their own particular needs. Such programs provide all employees equal access to a host of benefits. Moreover, they work to empower employees by providing workers with the resources needed to balance their work and family commitments. Workers gain some control over their own jobs—what they do, how they do it, and when.

Here are some examples of family-friendly benefits intended to help working families balance work and family responsibilities:

Day/Child Care Benefits. One of the most critical problems facing working parents today is quality care for their children. This concern will only be magnified in the coming years with the changing makeup of the workforce. Responding to this issue will be one of the greatest challenges for public and private sector employers. There is a variety of programs employers can offer to help employees care for their children during the working day. These include on-site or near-site child care centers; programs to facilitate access to care at the homes of child care providers (referred to as "family care"), resource and referral programs, efforts to develop child care resources in local communities, payment of part of employees' child care costs, and child care consortiums with other employers.

Although on-site or near-site child care facilities tend to be most desirable, relatively few public or private sector employers provide for such benefits. In fact, a survey conducted by the Census Bureau found that in 1993, almost half (48 percent) of all preschool-age children were primarily cared for by relatives. And the U.S. Merit Systems Protection Board found that only sixty-five on-site child care centers were serving civilian federal employees, thus accommodating an extremely small proportion of employee needs.[23]

Some employers in the private sector, faced with tight labor markets, have not provided on-site child care but have allowed workers to bring their children to the office and care for them while doing their jobs. Although this arrangement may not be desirable on a large scale, it certainly is a creative way for employers to retain valuable employees.[24] As we move into the next century, one of the biggest challenges for employers will be to assist working parents to locate high-quality, reliable, low-cost child care.

Family Leave Benefits. In almost 70 percent of families in the United States, both parents work. Almost 30 percent of all families are headed by a single parent, nearly 90 percent of them women.[25] In short, people with families work, and, given the changing values of American society, they are looking for ways to better balance their work and family responsibilities. To the extent that government employers recognize this and account for it in their benefits packages, they can effectively satisfy a growing need among American workers.

The Family and Medical Leave Act (FMLA) of 1993 requires public and private sector employers to provide employees up to twelve weeks of unpaid leave per year for (1) the birth or adoption of a child, (2) an employee's medical condition, and (3) an employee's need to care for a child, spouse, or parent who has a serious health condition. The FMLA applies to employees with one year of service who worked 1,250 hours during the year targeted for leave, and whose employer has fifty or more workers. The FMLA does not require employers to provide paid leave. Table 5.7 provides a comparison of family leave policy in the United States with that of other nations. As the table shows, other nations are more generous with family leave programs, not only offering leave for longer periods but, in every nation other than the United States, offering leave that is paid, either by the government or the individual's employer.

The federal government has made a host of efforts to help working families balance their work and family demands.[26] For example, in 1994, the Federal Employees Family Friendly Leave Act (FEFFLA) was enacted, which allows federal employees to use their sick leave to care for family members or for bereavement. More specifically, the FEFFLA authorizes covered full-time employees to use a total of up to forty hours (five workdays) of sick leave per year to (1) give care or otherwise attend to a family member having an illness, injury, or other condition that, if an employee had such a condition, would justify the use of sick leave by the

TABLE 5.7   Family Leave Policies Around the World

Country	Duration of Leave (Weeks)	Number of Paid Weeks/ Percentage of Normal Pay (Paid by govt. and/or employer)
Brazil	12	12 weeks/100
Canada	17–41	15 weeks/60
France	18	16 weeks/90
Germany	14–26 (3 years/parental leave)	14–19 weeks/100
Italy	8–20 (3 years/ill child)	8–20 weeks/80
Japan	12	12 weeks/60
Mexico	12–24	12 weeks/100 12 weeks/50
Sweden	12–52	38 weeks/90
United Kingdom	11–40	6 weeks/90 12 weeks/standard rate
USA	12	12 weeks/unpaid
Venezuela	18	18 weeks/100

Source: Suzanne M. Crampton and Jitendra M. Mishra, "Family and Medical Leave Legislation: Organizational Policies and Strategies," *Public Personnel Management,* Fall 1995, p. 285.

employee or (2) make arrangements for or attend the funeral of a family member.

Some of the benefit programs that states and localities have developed go beyond the FMLA. For example, New York State's family sick leave policy not only provides leave with pay under certain circumstances but also has broader coverage (e.g., children over eighteen years of age are covered under New York State's policy but are excluded from coverage under the FMLA). Table 5.8 compares the benefits of New York's leave policy and the FMLA's.

Also see Table 5.9, which illustrates state and local government employees' use of family leave programs. As the data show, as compared

TABLE 5.8   Leave Benefits Under New York State's Program and the Family Medical Leave Act (FMLA)

Relationship to Employee	New York State Family Sick Leave	FMLA
Spouse	Yes	Yes
Spouse equivalent	Yes, if residing with employee	No, regardless of residence
Child under 18 or impaired	Yes	Yes
Child over 18 or not impaired	Yes	No
Foster child	Yes, if residing with employee	Yes, regardless of residence
Parents	Yes	Yes
Parent-in-law	Yes	No
Foster parent	Yes, if residing with employee	Yes, regardless of residence
Other relatives (e.g., grandparents) or in-laws	Yes	No

Source: New York State Department of Civil Service, *Policy Bulletin* 93-06, 1993.

with other types of leave, a very high percentage of state and local government employees participate in unpaid family leave programs.

Although both the federal and state family leave laws have helped many working families meet the demands of balancing work and family, low-income households can't afford to take unpaid time off from work to care for a new baby, a sick child, or an elderly parent or grandparent who needs special care. This problem is exacerbated as more and more single mothers leave the welfare rolls for low-paying jobs that don't tend to offer child care benefits. The National Partnership for Women and Families, a nonprofit, nonpartisan organization that uses public education and advocacy to promote fairness in the workplace, quality health care, and policies that help women and men meet the dual demands of work and family, launched the Campaign for Family Leave Benefits in June 1999, a lobbying program to encourage legislators, policymakers, and other key officials in state and federal governments to make family

TABLE 5.9   State and Local Government Employees' Use of Leave
Programs, 1994 (Percentages)

Type of Leave	Employee Use of Leave
Paid Time Off	
Holidays	73
Vacations	66
Personal	38
Military	75
Jury Duty	94
Funeral	62
Sick	94
Family	4
Paid Time Off	
Family	93

Source: U.S. Department of Labor, Bureau of Labor Statistics, *Employee
Benefits in State and Local Government, 1994.*
http://stats.bls.gov/opub/cwc/cwchome.htm.

and medical leave affordable for every American family by providing
some income for people on leave. The National Partnership's goal is to
make family leave a reality for more people by making it less of a financial risk to take time off for childbirth or caring for a sick child or elderly
relative.[27]

Domestic Violence Leave.   Twenty-five to thirty percent of battered women
cite abuse as the reason they lose their jobs. In addition, 50–55 percent of
abused women miss work because of abuse, and 60 percent report being
late for work due to abuse. The National Partnership for Women and
Families has been a strong proponent of leave for victims of domestic violence. It urges employers to consider leave programs for domestic vio-

lence, since such victims require time away from work for a host of reasons including the following: (1) going to court to obtain protection
orders against batterers, (2) seeking medical treatment, (3) seeking new
living arrangements, and (4) seeking child care.

The U.S. Office of Personnel Management (OPM) also provides
resources for employees who are victims of domestic violence. In addition, it assists federal organizations in developing a wide range of tools
for protecting threatened employees and their colleagues, and for helping
them negotiate difficult transitions with minimum disruption to their life
and work. The resources, leave programs, and protections available
under the federal personnel system are important in the government's
overall efforts to assist victims and potential victims of domestic violence.

Alternative Work Schedules. Flextime and credit hours are examples of
flexible or compressed work schedules. They are intended to allow
employees to adjust the traditional fixed schedule of working eight hours
a day, five days a week. For example, an employee can elect to work four
ten-hour days per week or adjust the starting and ending times of the
eight-hour workday in order to accommodate family needs and commitments. Under such a scenario, an employee could work from 10:00 A.M.
to 6:00 P.M., instead of the traditional nine-to-five schedule.

Such programs grant employees some control over their work schedules, and studies by the GAO, OPM, and other agencies have shown that
flexible work schedules can positively influence the lives of federal
employees and also improve productivity. Table 5.10 provides data on the
percentage of employees in the public and private sectors with flexible
work schedules.

As Table 5.10 shows, alternative work schedules are very popular in
the federal government today. Aside from the entertainment and recre-
ation industry in the private sector, federal employees represent the
second largest cohort of workers relying on flexible work schedules. The
federal government remains committed to the use of alternative work
schedules as a way for federal employees to balance their work and family needs.

Flexiplace. Flexiplace refers to a flexible workplace, whereby the
employee's work site is located away from the primary principal office.
Work-at-home, telecommuting, and teleworking are examples of paid
employment away from the traditional work site. Workers perform the

TABLE 5.10 Flexible Schedules: Full-Time Wage and Salary Workers by Industry, May 1997 (Thousands)

Industry	Both sexes			Men			Women		
	Total Workers	With Flexible Schedules		Total Workers	With Flexible Schedules		Total Workers	With Flexible Schedules	
		Number	% of total		Number	% of total		Number	% of total
Private sector	75,612	21,795	28.8	45,023	13,284	29.5	30,589	8,511	27.8
Goods-producing industries	25,925	6,033	23.3	19,458	4,640	23.8	6,466	1,393	21.5
Agriculture	1,492	448	30.0	1,265	373	29.5	227	74	32.8
Mining	541	122	22.6	473	106	22.4	68	16	NA
Construction	5,389	1,218	22.6	4,974	1,086	21.8	415	132	31.8
Manufacturing	18,503	4,245	22.9	12,747	3,074	24.1	5,756	1,170	20.3
Durable goods	11,179	2,572	23.0	8,148	1,944	23.9	3,031	629	20.7
Nondurable goods	7,324	1,673	22.8	4,599	1,131	24.6	2,725	542	19.9
Service-producing industries	49,687	15,763	31.7	25,565	8,644	33.8	24,122	7,118	29.5
Transportation and public utilities	6,088	1,669	27.4	4,518	1,215	26.9	1,570	454	28.9
Wholesale trade	3,969	1,281	32.3	2,854	979	34.3	1,115	302	27.1
Retail trade	12,111	3,745	30.9	6,812	1,988	29.2	5,299	1,757	33.2
Eating and drinking places	3,135	987	31.5	1,758	497	28.2	1,377	490	35.6
Finance, insurance and real estate	5,857	2,096	35.8	2,288	1,028	44.9	3,569	1,068	29.9
Services	21,662	6,971	32.2	9,094	3,434	37.8	12,568	3,537	28.1
Private households	391	148	37.7	42	27	(2)	350	120	34.4
Business, automobile, and repair	5,060	1,607	31.8	3,319	1,118	33.7	1,740	489	28.1

TABLE 5.10   *(continued)*

	Both sexes			Men			Women		
	Total Workers	With Flexible Schedules		Total Workers	With Flexible Schedules		Total Workers	With Flexible Schedules	
		Number	% of total		Number	% of total		Number	% of total
Services (cont.)									
Personal, except private household	1,627	522	32.1	749	227	30.3	878	295	33.7
Entertainment and recreation	1,051	397	37.8	619	231	37.3	432	167	38.5
Professional services	13,497	4,286	31.8	4,336	1,820	42.0	9,161	2,465	26.9
Forestry and fisheries	36	11	NA	29	11	NA	7	-	-
Government	14,937	3,236	21.7	7,050	1,668	23.7	7,887	1,568	19.9
Federal	2,828	977	34.5	1,621	535	33.0	1,208	442	36.6
State	4,125	1,214	29.4	1,856	606	32.7	2,270	608	26.8
Local	7,983	1,046	13.1	3,573	527	14.8	4,410	519	11.8

NA: Percentage not shown where base is less than 75,000.

Source: U.S. Bureau of Labor Statistics, http://stats.bls.gov/news.release/flex.t02.htm.

work at home or at a satellite office and communicate with their offices via computer or telephone. Rapid technological and information changes have given way to an increasing number of flexiplace arrangements, not only in the private sector but in the public sector as well. Indeed, telecommuting has been occurring worldwide for more than twenty years. The use of high-tech telecommunications and computers make it easier for workers to perform their work at home, thereby allowing them to care for children or elderly relatives.

The Federal Flexible Workplace Program was established in the early 1990s as a pilot program to gain experience with flexiplace arrangements. The program allows federal employees to perform or telecommunicate their work away from the office—at home or at a satellite work site—for an agreed-on part of their workweek. The federal government considers the flexible workplace program appropriate in a variety of circumstances, including temporary and permanent arrangements, as well as short- and long-term periods. According to the U.S. Office of Personnel Management, the following represent examples of acceptable flexible workplace arrangements:

1. Part-time working at home while recovering from illness or injury
2. Taking care of family members for a variety of reasons
3. Reducing time on worker's compensation
4. Maternity/paternity leave
5. Accommodating the physically disabled
6. Project work
7. Intermittent need for quiet
8. Occasional need for concentration on an issue
9. Writing work
10. Temporary closure of main work site for repairs/renovation or weather
11. Regular and recurring work for one or more days per pay period or week[28]

Only one-tenth of 1 percent of the federal workforce (or 2,000 federal employees) was participating in flexiplace as of this writing. Expanding telecommuting opportunities is particularly important in the federal sector because, as the MSPB found in a survey of federal employees, telecommuting was one of the most important family-friendly programs, despite lack of availability. In fact, the MSPB survey showed that 44 percent of the workers who consider telecommuting to be important are more likely to leave their jobs because of its lack of availability.[29]

In 1999, President Clinton directed the U.S. Office of Personnel Management (OPM) to establish the Interagency Family-Friendly Workplace Working Group to promote, evaluate, and exchange information on federal family-friendly workplace initiatives. Heads of federal agencies were asked to appoint a family-friendly work/life coordinator to serve as a member of the working group. These individuals, along with the existing OPM Family-Friendly Workplace Advocacy Office, are responsible for providing federal employees with information about child and elder care community resources, making employees aware of the full range of human resources flexibility programs available to them, and establishing and promoting parent and elder care support groups and on-site programs for nursing mothers.

In sum, benefit programs to accommodate the needs and interests of women are vital if government agencies are to effectively recruit and *retain* women employees and ensure that they are motivated and productive. As already noted, leave programs help to empower employees, giving them some control over their work life as it pertains to or affects their family responsibilities and obligations.

Training and Development

Training, development, and education are key in preparing the workforce for diversity. This suggests not only training managers, supervisors, and workers for the realities of today's and tomorrow's workforce, but it also calls for preparing women for the demands of the changing nature of work.

Training and Development in Technology. As suggested in Chapter 4, women and people of color may not have been provided the opportunities to be adequately prepared for the high-tech jobs in the workplace, despite such calls by demographers and labor specialists, most notably in the Hudson Institute's *Workforce 2000*, which was released in 1987.[30] The calls for training women in computer science and technology continue to be made.

As shown in Table 5.11, women continue to lag in terms of educational attainment in such fields as computer and information sciences and engineering, at the bachelor's, master's, and doctoral levels. On the other hand, they are well represented in such traditional fields as educa-

TABLE 5.11   Degrees Conferred by Field, Level of Degree, and Gender, 1996–1997

		Men		Women	
Field of study	*Total degrees*	*Total*	*Percent*	*Total*	*Percent*
Bachelor's Degrees					
Business management and admin. services	221875	114,500	51.6	107,375	48.4
Social sciences and history	124,891	64,115	51.3	60,776	48.7
Education	105,233	26,271	25.0	78,962	75.0
Health professions and related sciences	85,631	15,877	18.5	69,754	81.5
Psychology	74,191	19,379	26.1	54,812	73.9
Biological sciences/life sciences	63,975	29,470	46.1	34,505	53.9
Engineering	61,185	50,058	81.8	11,127	18.2
Visual & performing arts	50,083	20,729	41.4	29,354	58.6
English language and literature/letters	49,345	16,531	33.5	32,814	66.5
Communications	47,230	19,412	41.1	27,818	58.9
Master's degrees					
Education	110,087	25,806	23.4	84,281	76.6
Business management and admin. services	96,923	59,235	61.1	37,688	38.9
Health professions and related sciences	35,958	7,702	21.4	28,256	78.6
Engineering	25,787	21,120	81.9	4,667	18.1
Public administration and services	24,781	6,957	28.1	17,824	71.9
Social sciences and history	14,787	8,830	53.0	5,957	47.0
Psychology	14,353	3,852	26.8	10,501	73.2
Visual and performing arts	10,627	4,470	42.1	6,157	57.9
Computer and information services	10,098	7,248	71.8	2,850	28.2
English language and literature/letters	7,722	2,733	35.4	4,989	64.6
Doctor's degrees					
Education	6,751	2,512	37.2	4,239	62.8
Engineering	6,201	5,438	87.7	763	12.3
Biological sciences/life sciences	4,812	2,738	56.9	2,074	43.1
Physical sciences	4,467	3,438	77.0	1,029	23.0
Psychology	4,053	1,350	33.3	2,703	66.7
Social sciences and history	3,989	2,479	62.1	1,510	37.9
Health professions and related sciences	2,672	1,176	44.0	1,496	56.0
English language and literature/letters	1,575	670	42.5	905	57.5
Theological studies/religious vocations	1,395	1,143	81.9	252	18.1
Business management and admin services	1,334	946	70.9	388	29.1

Source: U.S. Department of Education, National Center for Education Statistics, "Integrated Postsecondary Education Data System," 1997.

tion and psychology. Obviously, the responsibility to correct these disparities goes well beyond the work setting. Socialization is in large part responsible for patterns of choice and for the grooming or molding of women for certain educational and employment endeavors as opposed to others (e.g., those considered nontraditional for women). Notwithstanding, to the extent that government employers seek to attract and retain quality employees, providing on-the-job training programs is but one effort that could address the skills gap that currently exists.

As noted earlier, ensuring that women have the physical skills to perform such nontraditional work as firefighting and sanitation is also critical.[31] It's not a question of, Why would a woman want to be a garbage collector or a corrections officer? but rather, Do women have the opportunities to enter the vocation or profession of their choice, be it blue-collar or "pink-collar"? Uniformed service jobs pay a very competitive rate, making them attractive to women who would otherwise go into pink-collar jobs.

Importantly, high-tech jobs go well beyond word processing. Although word processing has revolutionized the workplace, it continues to be associated with clerical or women's work. Some have argued that a high premium has not been placed on word processing, unlike other computer-related jobs, and that the implications of technological change for women's work has not yet been fully addressed.[32]

Managing diversity includes ensuring that women have the tools and skills needed to perform the new jobs created by technological and information advances in the workplace, as well as the skills needed to perform jobs that continue to require physical strength. Government employers' ability to attract and retain women may depend on it.

Training to Combat Negative Stereotypes. A prominent organizational theorist, Robert Golembiewski, observed that traditional bureaucratic structures "literally ooze conventional 'masculinity.'"[33] Golembiewski points out that good managers have traditionally been seen as "aggressive, competitive, firm . . . [and] not feminine. . . . Men are portrayed as more competent and task-oriented, while women tend to be seen as warmer and more expressive."[34] Although these images are at the heart of the culture of organizations, they also speak to the commonly held stereotypes surrounding gender.

Table 5.12 provides a list of stereotypes typically associated with women. Such stereotypes impede efforts to successfully manage diver-

TABLE 5.12   Commonly Held Gender Stereotypes

Gender	Stereotypes
Women	Catty and bitchy; not serious about careers; emotionally out of control; sleep their way up career ladder; indecisive and less competent
Men	Think they know everything; macho; suppress their feelings; prefer subservient women; nurturing men are wimps

Source: Adapted from Marilyn Loden and Judy B. Rosener *Workforce America!* Homewood, Ill.: Business One Irwin (1991).

sity in the workplace and, to the extent these stereotypes are held by high-level executives in government, they also hinder the employment opportunities available to women. As stressed in Chapter 4, training programs to combat these negative stereotypes are critical to developing harmonious, productive workforces. Some government employers have also developed training programs to foster multicultural awareness among managers and employees. Such programs can ultimately improve the overall management of diversity in the workplace. The key to the success of such programs is breaking down negative stereotypes.

Educating Workers on "Who Is Really Qualified for the Job."   As discussed in Chapter 4, government managers and workers will also need to be educated to understand the biases in how people's competencies and qualifications are judged. Assuming that women are unqualified for their jobs based on culturally biased indicators of performance (e.g., merit exams), or culturally biased validation scales will need to be corrected.

A good illustration can be seen in the reporting of the U.S. Supreme Court's decision in *Johnson v. Santa Clara County Transportation Agency* (1987).[35] It may be recalled that *Johnson* involved the promotion of a female applicant, Diane Joyce, to the position of road dispatcher in the county's transportation agency. Paul Johnson, another applicant for the position, filed suit charging that he was denied the promotion based on his sex in violation of Title VII of the Civil Rights Act. One of the issues raised in the case was the difference in their test scores in an oral interview. Diane Joyce earned a score of seventy-three, while Paul Johnson earned a seventy-five.

The U.S. Supreme Court ruled in favor of Joyce on grounds that the county hired her pursuant to a voluntarily developed affirmative action plan aimed at correcting gender imbalances in traditionally segregated job categories. Such a program, according to the Court majority, is legal under Title VII. Despite this opinion, the media, in reporting the case, exacerbated already heated tensions around affirmative action. The *New York Times*, for example, in its opening paragraph, said that "the Supreme Court ruled today that employers may sometimes favor women and members of minorities over better-qualified men and whites in hiring and promoting to achieve better balance in their work forces."[36] In addition, the Supreme Court's dissenting opinion in *Johnson* said that the decision would "loose a flood of 'less qualified' minorities and women upon the work force."[37]

Efforts to combat these views and beliefs are obviously important if programs and policies to manage diversity are to prove successful.

Diversity Means Inclusion, NOT Exclusion.   As noted in Chapter 4, managers and supervisors must be trained in order to develop a managerial style based on *inclusion* rather than exclusion. Researchers and employment analysts have found that managers, when faced with pressure to diversify their workforces, are more apt to hire or promote white women as opposed to women or men of color. Part of this problem stems from the fact that those who possess the authority to make hiring and promotion decisions have historically tended to be white and mostly male. Thus, if there are efforts or pressures to diversify, "cloning," at least by race, was the outcome. To the degree that the complexion of higher-levels of government become more diverse, a major part of this problem can potentially be solved. In the meantime, managers must be trained to recognize that inclusion, from a diversity perspective, goes beyond hiring and promoting only white women.

Creating a System of Pay Equity

As noted earlier, Secretary of Labor Alexis M. Herman has stated that even when women are able to advance into upper-level, senior management positions in the workplace, they continue to face the barrier of disparate pay. In general, women routinely earn less than their male counterparts. Despite the Equal Pay Act of 1963, which requires women and men to be paid "equal pay for equal work," women continue to earn about seventy-three cents for every dollar earned by a male.[38]

TABLE 5.13   Median Salaries by Race and Gender in State and Local Governments, 1985, 1989, 1997

	MEN	WOMEN
1985	$22,332	$17,262
1989	$26,070	$20,631
1997	$34,575	$27,864

Source: Calculated from unpublished U.S. Equal Employment Opportunity Commission reports, and U.S. Equal Employment Opportunity Commission, *Job Patterns for Minorities and Women in State and Local Governments*, 1989, 1990, 1997.

Table 5.13 compares the median salaries of men and women in state and local government jobs for three time periods. Without ascribing the differences to any particular factor, the data show that women consistently earn less than males in state and local government jobs.

"Equal pay for comparable worth" was once at the forefront of the pay equity debate. This term refers to paying equal wages to women and men who perform different work that is of *comparable value* to an employer. The concern revolves around the fact that women and men perform different jobs, but the jobs performed by women tend to be valued less and therefore paid less. Women working as nurses, librarians, and secretaries tend to be paid less than men in jobs requiring comparable skill and effort and of equal value to their employers. For example, a secretary and a maintenance worker perform markedly different tasks, but a review of wage schedules often showed maintenance workers (who tend to be men) receiving higher wages than the secretaries (who tend to be women).

Comparable worth advocates argued that an inventory of the skills, knowledge, and qualifications for the jobs could be compared to determine the worth of the job to the employer. Ultimately a more equitable salary scale for all workers would be identified.

There is very little activity around comparable worth as a strategy for achieving pay equity for women because of a critical court ruling in the mid-1980s. In *American Federation of State, County, and Municipal Employees*

(AFSCME) v. State of Washington (1985),[39] the U.S. Court of Appeals for the Ninth Circuit virtually killed comparable worth on substantive grounds. In this decision, the court held that the state of Washington could not be in violation of Title VII if it based its wages on prevailing market rates, even if the outcome meant lower salaries for women. The court, subscribing to the free market theory, ruled that the state did not create the market disparity, and "neither law nor logic deems the free market system a suspect enterprise."

In 1999, the AFL-CIO launched a new comparable worth initiative. The initiative includes the planned introduction of comparable worth legislation in twenty-two states. As part of this push, the federation and the Institute for Women's Policy Research released a new report on the gender pay gap entitled *Equal Pay for Working Families.* According to the report, women and men who work in traditionally female-dominated jobs lose $113 billion annually due to "unequal pay."

Despite the case law and general resistance to comparable worth, a small number of states and localities continue to rely on it to redress pay inequities. For example, Minnesota state law, which continues to be enforced, requires all public jurisdictions, such as cities, counties, and school districts, to eliminate any sex-based wage inequities in compensation. The state relies on a method of "pay equity," which seeks to pay women and men equal wages for jobs requiring comparable levels of expertise. The state offers this example of how "pay equity" would be applied to eliminate wage inequities:[40]

Job	Job Evaluation Rating	Salary (to be corrected)
Delivery van driver (mostly men)	117 points	$1,900 per month
Clerk typist (mostly women)	117 points	$1,400 per month

Conclusion

As women continue to increase their share of public and private sector jobs, employers are challenged to create a work environment that combats views and policies that negatively affect women, an environment that creates opportunities for women employees to be satisfied, productive members of the workforce. This chapter outlined some of the strategies that could be relied on to effectively manage gender diversity in the workplace.

Notes

1. See "Mapping Out a Strategy to Shatter Glass Ceilings and Glass Walls," 2000, http://www.advancingwomen.com/wk_glassceiling2.html.

2. The glass ceiling has also been a problem for men of color, but this chapter will address the concept as it pertains to women only.

3. The U.S. Department of Labor, *A Report on the Glass Ceiling Initiative* (Washington, D.C., 1991).

4. The U.S. Merit System Protection Board (MSPB), *A Question of Equity: Women and the Glass Ceiling* (Washington, D.C., 1992).

5. See, for example, MSPB, *A Question of Equity;* and U.S. Department of Labor, *Report on the Glass Ceiling Initiative,* p. 5.

6. See New York State Center for Women in Government, *Bulletin,* 1991–1992, pp. 1–2.

7. Secretary of Labor Alexis M. Herman, as quoted in "Mapping Out a Strategy."

8. See, for example, Samuel Krislov and David H. Rosenbloom, *Representative Bureaucracy and the American Political System* (New York: Praeger, 1981); and James D. Slack, "Affirmative Action and City Managers: Attitudes Toward Recruitment of Women," *Public Administration Review* 47 (1987): 199–206.

9. See the large body of literature on representative bureaucracy, particularly as it addresses active representation. The concept of representative bureaucracy is premised on the notion that the needs and interests of women, African Americans, Latinos, Asians, American Indians, and other groups in not just the workforce but also the broader society will be more effectively served if the upper policymaking levels of public bureaucracies include these persons. For discussions, see, for example, Kenneth J. Meier, "Representative Bureaucracy: A Theoretical and Empirical Exposition," in James Perry, ed., *Research in Public Administration* (Greenwich, Conn.: JAI Press, 1993), pp. 1–35; Krislov and Rosenbloom, *Representative Bureaucracy;* and Joseph N. Cayer and Lee Sigelman, "Minorities and Women in State and Local Government: 1973–1975," *Public Administration Review* 40 (1980): 443–450.

10. See, for example, *Berkman v. New York City,* 536 F. Supp. 177 (1982); aff'd., 705 F.2d 584 (2d Cir. 1983); and *Berkman v. New York City,* 812 F.2d 52 (2d Cir. 1987); *cert. denied,* 108 S. Ct. 146 (1987).

11. Concurrent validity is actually a strategy for achieving criterion-related validity which seeks to demonstrate that the test scores of persons hired for a job later correlate with their job performance.

12. See Norma M. Riccucci, "Merit, Equity, and Test Validity: A New Look at an Old Problem," *Administration and Society,* May 1991, pp. 74–93.

13. See, for example, *Berkman v. New York City,* 580 F. Supp. 226 (1983).

14. Felice N. Schwartz, "Management Women and the New Facts of Life," *Harvard Business Review,* January-February 1989, pp. 65–76.

15. MSPB, *Sexual Harassment in the Federal Workplace* (Washington, D.C., 1995).

16. Ibid.

17. *Meritor Savings Bank v. Vinson*, 106 S. Ct. 2399 (1986) at p. 2403.

18. *Harris v. Forklift Systems, Inc.*, 114 S. Ct. 367 (1993) at p. 369.

19. *Oncale v. Sundowner Offshore Services*, 523 U.S. 75 (1998).

20. *Faragher v. City of Boca Raton*, 118 S. Ct. 2275 (1998).

21. *Burlington Industries v. Ellerth*, 118 S. Ct. 2257 (1998).

22. See, for example, a report by the Family Caregiver Alliance, http://www.caregiver.org/factsheets/caregiver_stats.html.

23. See MSPB, *Balancing Work Responsibilities and Family Needs: The Federal Civil Service Response* (Washington, D.C., 1991).

24. See "A Bit of Burping Is Allowed, If It Keeps Parents on the Job," *New York Times*, December 4, 2000, pp. A1, A22.

25. See Soonhee Kim, "The Effects of Family Leave Policy on Employees and Agencies in New York State Government" (Ph.D. diss., State University of New York at Albany, 1998).

26. See MSPB, *Balancing Work Responsibilities and Family Needs.*

27. See www.nationalpartnership.org.

28. See http://www.usbr.gov/recman/hrm/hrm11–01.htm.

29. MSPB, "Issues of Merit," *MSPB Newsletter*, December 2000.

30. *Workforce 2000* (Indianapolis: Hudson Institute, 1987).

31. *Workforce 2020* (Indianapolis: Hudson Institute, 1997) makes the point that technological advances are making physical strength an irrelevant job attribute in private sector workforces. However, this is not necessarily the case in the public sector, as indicated by uniformed services jobs.

32. See, for example, Belinda Probert and Bruce Wilson, eds., *Pink Collar Blues: Work, Gender, and Technology* (Australia: Melbourne University Press, 1993).

33. Robert T. Golembiewski, *Managing Diversity in Organizations* (Tuscaloosa: University of Alabama Press, 1995), p. 64.

34. Ibid.

35. *Johnson v. Santa Clara County Transportation Agency*, 107 S. Ct. 1442 (1987).

36. S. Taylor Jr., "Supreme Court, 6–3, Extends Preferences in Employment for Women and Minorities," *New York Times*, March 26, 1987, p. A1.

37. *Johnson v. Santa Clara County Transportation Agency* (1987) at p. 1457 n. 17.

38. See, for example, http://www.feminist.com/fairpay/epd.htm; http://www.epf.org/pay_equity.htm.

39. 770 F.2d 1401 (9th Cir. 1985).

40. See http://www.doer.state.mn.us/lr-peqty/ab-peqty.htm.

Additional Reading

Carnevale, Anthony Patrick, and Susan Carol Stone. *The American Mosaic*. New York: McGraw-Hill, 1995.

Daly, Alfrieda, ed. *Workplace Diversity Issues and Perspectives*. Washington, D.C.: National Association of Social Workers Press, 1998.

Dobbs, Matti F. "Managing Diversity: Lessons from the Private Sector." *Public Personnel Management,* Fall 1996, pp. 351–367.

Dolan, Jennifer A., and Leigh Giles-Brown. "Realizing the Benefits of Diversity: A Wake-Up Call." *Public Manager,* Spring 1999, pp. 51–55.

Ferguson, Kathy E. *The Feminist Case Against Bureaucracy.* Philadelphia: Temple University Press, 1984.

Henderson, George. *Cultural Diversity in the Workplace.* Westport, Conn.: Quorum, 1994.

Kelly, Rita Mae, and Jane Bayes. *Comparable Worth, Pay Equity, and Public Policy.* Westport, Conn.: Greenwood, 1988.

Lee, Robert D., Jr., and Paul S. Greenlaw. "A Legal Perspective on Sexual Harassment." In Carolyn Ban and Norma M. Riccucci, eds., *Public Personnel Management: Current Concerns, Future Challenges.* 2d ed. New York: Longman, 1997.

Loden, Marilyn. *Implementing Diversity.* Chicago: Irwin Professional Publishing, 1996.

Lynch, Frederick R. *The Diversity Machine.* New York: Free Press, 1997.

Roberts, Gary. "An Inventory of Family-Friendly Benefit Practices in Small New Jersey Local Governments." *Review of Public Personnel Administration,* Spring 2000, pp. 50–62.

Stivers, Camilla. *Gender Images in Public Administration: Legitimacy and the Administrative State.* Newbury Park, Calif.: Sage, 1993.

Tayeb, Monir H. *The Management of a Multicultural Workforce.* New York: Wiley, 1996.

Woolridge, Blue. "Changing Demographics in the Work Force: Implications for the Use of Technology in Public Organizations." *Public Productivity and Management Review,* 17, 1994, pp. 371–386.

6

Managing the Multigenerational Workplace

The American workforce is becoming increasingly diverse not only in terms of race, ethnicity, and gender, but also in terms of age. *Workforce 2020* has predicted that the oldest of the baby boomers—those born between 1945 and 1965 will begin to reach age sixty-five in 2010, and that there will be as many workers of "retirement age" as there are twenty- to thirty-five-year-olds.[1] As baby boomers continue to age and as the digital or "dot.com" generation adds to the workforce mix, challenges arise for managing cross-generational government work settings. Different generations in the same work space can create tensions around job performance, technological faculties, and overall capabilities. With the likelihood of retirement age being pushed up—the Social Security retirement age is already scheduled to increase to sixty-seven by the year 2027[2]—the range in age of government workers will become wider.

Although multiple generations have characterized the workplace in the past, generational "mixing" was often rare. Social and physical separations created by the work itself, as well as organizational structures, kept the generations from intermingling. However, in today's informational and technological work world, younger workers sometimes supervise older workers, and participative leadership styles, which are more prevalent and in demand today for a variety of reasons, require, indeed necessitate, intergenerational mixing.[3]

As government employers develop policies for managing diversity, age is an important characteristic that must be factored into these programs. This chapter begins by looking at government workforces by age groups. It then examines the various strategies that have been or could be relied upon for effectively managing age diversity in public sector employment.

The Cross-Generational Mix of
Workers in Public Employment

Table 6.1 presents data on workers at the federal, state, and local levels of government by age. Several interesting observations can be made from these data. One of the most important is that there is a wide span of workers in government, ranging from sixteen to over seventy-five years of age. In addition, as the table shows, in every category of government employees, there is a greater number of workers who are sixty-five and older as compared to the age cohort of sixteen to nineteen years. The one exception is for state employees, where the numbers are very similar. The data also show that the largest cohort of government employees at all levels is forty-five to fifty-four. The next highest age cohort is thirty-five to forty-four.

It is also interesting to note that there are relatively large numbers of government workers in all levels from ages fifty-five to sixty-four as well as from twenty-five to thirty-four years. Finally, the data in Table 6.1 also show that many government employees continue to work beyond the age of seventy. Even though federal employees may be eligible to retire, they are remaining on the job.[4]

Table 6.2 provides data on the age and race of government workers at the federal, state, and local levels. These data are presented to illustrate the range in age of workers, and also the diversity in terms of race.

Tables 6.3 and 6.4 provide data on the age range of federal workers as well as the average age of federal government workers by department. These snapshots of government workforces at the federal as well as state and local levels indicate the multigenerational nature of public sector organizations. As noted earlier, government employers cannot overlook this important issue as they develop diversity programs to manage their workplaces.

Strategies for Managing Diversity in
the Multigenerational Workplace

The different generations at work can be roughly classified into at least four categories:

- *The veterans.* Born prior to World War II, these persons experienced the hardships of not only the war but the Depression as well.

TABLE 6.1 Employed Persons by Level of Government and Age, 1999 (Thousands)

Type of Worker	Total, 16 years and over	16–19 years			20–64 years						65 years and over			
		Total	16–17	18–19	Total	20–24	25–34	35–44	45–54	55–64	Total	65–69	70–74	75+
Total 16+	133,488	7,172	2,795	4,379	126,316	12,891	30,865	36,728	28,635	13,315	3,882	2,065	1,088	729
Private industries	102,420	6,533	2,542	3,992	95,887	11,246	25,071	27,901	19,944	9,227	2,497	1,361	715	421
Government	18,903	338	115	224	18,565	1,041	3,653	5,430	5,711	2,275	454	271	105	79
Federal	3,243	34	10	24	3,210	106	541	1,020	1,062	413	67	41	10	15
State and local	15,659	304	104	200	15,355	935	3,112	4,410	4,649	1,862	387	230	94	63
State	5,232	106	13	92	5,126	401	1,007	1,484	1,525	604	105	60	26	19
Local	10,428	198	90	108	10,229	534	2,105	2,925	3,124	1,258	282	170	68	45

Source: U.S. Bureau of Labor Statistics, Labor Force Statistics from the Current Population Survey, http://www.bls.gov/cpshome.htm

TABLE 6.2   Employed Persons by Level of Government, Race, and Age, 1999 (thousands)

Type of Worker	Total	65 years and over			16–24 years	25–54 years	55–64 years
		65–69	70–74	75 years and over			
White, both sexes							
Private industries	2,232	1,206	651	374	14,970	60,799	8,088
Government	380	218	91	71	1,124	11,727	1,910
Federal	53	30	8	15	102	1,896	333
State and local	327	187	84	56	1,022	9,830	1,578
State	87	50	21	16	428	3,171	503
Local	241	138	62	40	595	6,660	1,075

Type of Worker	Total	65 years and over			16–24 years	25–54 years	55–64 years
		65–69	70–74	75 years and over			
African American, both sexes							
Private industries	185	105	43	37	2,061	8,468	765
Government	59	42	11	6	176	2,420	283
Federal	10	7	3	0	28	546	54
State and local	49	35	8	6	147	1,874	229
State	12	7	3	2	48	650	77
Local	37	28	5	4	99	1,224	152

Type of Worker	Total	65 years and over			16–24 years	25–54 years	55–64 years
		65–69	70–74	75 years and over			
Latino, both sexes							
Private industries	133	86	29	19	2,364	7,765	638
Government	21	11	5	4	151	1,127	148
Federal	3	2	1	-	13	175	19
State and local	18	9	4	4	138	952	109
State	6	3	-	3	49	258	24
Local	12	6	4	1	89	694	85

Source: U.S. Bureau of Labor Statistics, Labor Force Statistics from the Current Population Survey, http://www.bls.gov/cpshome.htm.

TABLE 6.3 Federal Civilian Employment Distribution within Selected Age-Groups, Executive Branch Agencies, Worldwide, September 30, 1998 (Men and Women Combined)

Agency	Total	Less than 31	31–40	41–44	45–49	50–54	55–59	60–64	65–69	70 and Greater
Total Executive Branch	1,804,591	173,894	450,566	245,888	348,202	334,102	168,144	73,688	20,853	9,254
Executive Office of the President	1,171	206	328	138	172	186	93	36	6	6
Executive Residence at the White House	84	5	20	16	10	11	11	8	1	2
Council of Economic Advisors	29	11	1	4	4	6	2	-	-	1
Council on Environmental Quality/ Office of Environmental Quality	18	3	5	3	6	1	-	-	-	-
National Security Council	41	7	16	4	4	6	2	1	1	-
Office of Administration	170	17	55	23	23	27	17	7	-	-
Office of Management and Budget	507	122	143	47	69	76	39	7	2	2
Office of National Drug Control Policy	123	16	31	15	14	30	10	6	1	-
Office of Science and Technology Policy	32	4	10	5	4	6	-	3	-	-
Office of the U.S. Trade Representative	167	21	47	21	38	23	12	4	1	-
Executive Departments	1,619,229	156,414	408,646	222,582	310,648	280,247	150,148	63,306	17,767	7,471
Department of Agriculture	107,689	15,644	24,779	15,418	20,325	16,489	9,045	3,974	1,326	689
Department of Commerce	39,917	5,961	9,948	4,454	6,109	5,812	3,686	1,768	725	454
Department of Defense	709,075	46,671	166,623	99,770	143,344	136,477	17,698	31,802	7,197	2,493
Department of the Army	230,815	14,363	51,519	32,558	47,807	45,662	24,945	10,484	2,516	961
Department of the Navy	193,902	12,092	46,526	28,113	39,763	36,529	19,846	8,578	1,807	648
Department of the Air Force	165,938	12,471	41,388	22,054	31,548	31,641	17,218	7,534	1,648	436

TABLE 6.3 (continued)

Agency	Total	Less than 31	31–40	41–44	45–49	50–54	55–59	60–64	65–69	70 and Greater
Department of Education	4,824	649	1,007	495	891	999	452	222	85	24
Department of Energy	16,148	879	3,404	2,162	3,580	3,472	1,820	630	156	45
Department of Health and Human Svc.	58,159	6,200	13,482	7,274	10,374	10,045	6,200	2,933	1,093	558
Department of Housing and Urban Dev.	9,983	585	1895	1,209	2,226	2,211	1,161	491	153	52
Department of the Interior	72,993	9,823	16,778	10,203	14,566	12,130	6,025	2,481	699	288
Department of Justice	122,580	24,155	47,398	15,639	16,669	11,798	4,576	1,610	498	237
Department of Labor	15,945	1,690	3,190	1,803	3,192	3,149	1,786	764	261	110
Department of State	15,605	1,365	4,108	2,045	2,817	2,594	1,497	728	236	215
Department of Transportation	68,842	4,450	20,235	9,417	10,801	10,876	5,743	2,403	705	212
Department of the Treasury	141,965	12,496	39,842	19,537	27,431	23,876	11,500	4,934	1,557	792
Department of Veterans Affairs	240,504	25,846	55,957	33,156	48,323	40,319	21,959	10,566	3,076	1,302
Independent Agencies	184,191	17,274	41,592	23,168	37,382	33,669	17,903	8,346	3,080	1,777
Advisory Commission on Intergovernmental Relations	19	-	-	3	2	5	1	5	3	-
Advisory Council on Historic Preservation	46	3	5	9	11	11	3	1	1	2
African Development Council	26	-	4	1	8	9	2	1	1	-
American Battle Monuments Comm.	51	1	1	2	6	11	12	12	6	-
Appalachian Regional Commission	10	-	2	2	2	2	1	1	-	-
Agricultural and Transportaion Barriers Compliance Board	44	4	13	6	12	3	5	1	-	-
Arctic Research Commission	10	-	1	-	-	1	3	2	1	2
Armed Forces Retirement Home	850	39	154	89	128	148	131	88	41	32

Source: U.S. Office of Personnel Management, http://www.opm.gov/feddata/demograp/demograp.htm#AgeData.

TABLE 6.4 Federal Civilian Employment Distribution by Sex and Minority Status, by Average Age and Average Years of Service, Executive Branch Agencies, Worldwide, September 30, 1998

Agency	Total	Men	Women	Total Minorities	Average Age			Average Years of Service		
					Men	Women	Minorities	Men	Women	Minorities
Total Executive Branch	1,834,591	1,003,341	801,250	534,801	45.2	43.3	42.9	15.7	13.7	13.9
Executive Office of the President	1,171	574	597	363	42.6	41.1	41.3	13.5	13.9	15.5
Executive Residence at the White House	84	64	20	30	45.0	51.4	49.1	17.6	12.6	16.3
Council of Economic Advisors	29	10	19	8	31.5	44.5	40.5	4.3	17.3	15.0
Council on Environmental Quality/ Office of Environmental Quality	18	8	10	1	39.0	40.9	43.0	9.8	11.5	14.0
National Security Council	41	17	24	11	38.2	42.2	42.1	12.1	16.3	21.4
Office of Administration	170	78	92	76	42.7	43.5	42.8	14.3	15.5	16.1
Office of Management and Budget	507	244	263	137	42.1	38.4	38.8	14.3	12.7	15.0
Office of National Drug Control Policy	123	65	58	42	45.0	42.2	41.5	8.5	12.2	12.4
Office of Science and Technology Policy	32	18	14	7	42.1	41.1	37.7	5.6	14.2	11.9
Office of the U.S. Trade Representative	167	70	97	51	43.1	42.1	41.3	15.1	16.1	17.6
Executive Departments	1,619,229	919,833	699,396	472,054	45.1	43.2	43.0	15.6	13.4	13.7
Department of Agriculture	107,689	62,261	45,428	22,719	44.3	41.6	40.8	15.3	11.6	12.1
Department of Commerce	39,917	20,335	18,582	10,688	43.9	42.7	40.3	13.9	11.1	11.3
Department of Defense	709,075	441,579	267,496	189,528	46.3	43.8	44.4	17.1	14.8	15.2
Department of the Army	230,815	144,622	86,193	60,209	46.6	44.1	44.5	17.0	15.4	15.0
Department of the Navy	193,902	131,373	62,529	54,743	46.1	43.5	44.6	17.7	15.1	15.8
Department of the Air Force	165,938	110,740	55,198	40,314	45.5	43.8	44.1	16.7	15.2	15.4

TABLE 6.4 (continued)

Agency	Total	Men	Women	Total Minorities	Average Age Men	Average Age Women	Average Age Minorities	Avg Yrs Service Men	Avg Yrs Service Women	Avg Yrs Service Minorities
Department of Education	4,824	1,841	2,983	2,183	47.0	42.9	43.3	15.2	14.3	15.5
Department of Energy	16,148	10,037	6,111	3,525	47.4	43.7	43.7	18.2	16.4	16.7
Department of Health and Human Svc.	58,159	23,383	34,776	24,160	47.0	43.5	42.8	13.9	12.9	12.7
Department of Housing and Urban Dev.	9,983	4,057	5,926	4,491	48.7	45.1	45.0	18.3	17.1	17.3
Department of the Interior	72,993	45,008	27,985	19,596	44.2	42.0	42.7	14.3	12.2	13.2
Department of Justice	122,580	75,071	47,509	39,114	38.9	39.4	38.1	11.4	11.3	11.1
Department of Labor	15,945	8,008	7,937	5,491	47.1	43.5	43.0	17.1	15.5	15.9
Department of State	15,605	8,446	7,159	3,629	45.7	43.8	43.5	16.2	13.1	15.5
Department of Transportation	68,842	46,993	17,849	13,174	44.7	42.4	42.8	17.3	15.1	16.4
Department of the Treasury	141,965	63,365	78,600	48,516	44.7	43.3	41.5	16.1	14.1	13.8
Department of Veterans Affairs	240,504	109,449	131,055	85,240	44.7	44.1	43.8	12.4	11.7	11.7
Independent Agencies	184,191	82,934	101,257	62,384	46.6	43.8	42.8	16.1	15.7	15.5
Advisory Commission on Intergovernmental Relations	19	16	3	1	58.0	42.7	42.0	1.4	1.7	3.0
Advisory Council on Historic Preservation	46	15	31	7	53.0	45.1	43.3	9.3	10.3	13.0
African Development Council	26	10	16	19	51.2	47.6	48.6	18.6	15.4	15.6
American Battle Monuments Comm.	51	46	5	5	56.1	48.8	46.0	15.1	20.4	14.4
Appalachian Regional Commission	10	5	5	2	50.2	44.0	43.5	18.4	16.6	21.0
Agricultural and Transportaion Barriers Compliance Board	44	21	23	10	44.3	42.0	34.1	6.1	8.5	8.3
Arctic Research Commission	10	9	1	-	59.8	56.0	-	3.6	31.0	-
Armed Forces Retirement Home	850	421	429	554	51.4	48.1	48.3	14.3	13.5	14.0

Source: U.S. Office of Personnel Management, http://www.opm.gov/feddata/demograp/demograp.htm#AgeData.

- *The baby boomers.* Persons born between 1945 and 1965 and raised in the era of opportunity and progress.
- *Generation Xers.* Persons born between 1965 and 1980, who came of age just as Ronald Reagan was elected to his first term in his two-term presidency.
- *Generation Nexters.* Persons born between 1980 and 2000, to the baby boomers and early Xers. They enter into the current high-tech world of work.[5]

The generations that occupy today's workplaces differ in terms of demographics, life experiences, politics, and even music. Their differences can be a source of strength and opportunity to an organization or a source of debilitating conflict. Understanding generational differences is perhaps key to successfully managing a multigenerational workforce and can ultimately lead to mutual respect, harmony, and synergy.[6] The following represents some of the strategies that public sector organizations can develop to better manage the intergenerational workplace.

Eradicating Age Discrimination

Age discrimination continues to exist in both the public and private sector workforces. The ability of government employers to combat, indeed refrain from, age discrimination will be a critical first step as they seek to manage workplaces in which the average age of public employees is on the increase.

In 1967, Congress enacted the Age Discrimination in Employment Act (ADEA), which made it illegal for private businesses to refuse to hire, discharge, or to otherwise discriminate against an individual, in compensation or privileges of employment, between the ages of forty and sixty-five. The act was amended in 1974 to apply to federal, state, and local governments.[7]

The ADEA was amended again in 1978 to raise to seventy the minimum mandatory retirement age for employees in private companies and state and local government. The 1978 amendment also banned forced retirement for federal employees at any age, except for federal law enforcement officers and firefighters.[8] Enforcement authority over the ADEA was originally vested in the Department of Labor but was transferred to the EEOC as part of the federal service reform of 1978.

The ADEA was again amended in 1986 to remove the upper age limit of seventy for all employees (private and state and local government) *except* for (1) firefighters; (2) high-level, policy-making executives who held such a position for at least two years and whose pension and benefits amount to at least $40,000 per year; (3) law enforcement officers; and (4) tenured university professors. The exceptions for law enforcement officers, firefighters, and tenured professors expired on December 31, 1993. However, in 1996, Congress once again amended the ADEA, reenacting the exemption to mandatory retirement for public safety officers (i.e., law enforcement officers and firefighters). Recognizing that age is not an accurate predictor of a public safety officer's fitness to serve, Congress also included a provision to the amendments, stating that a public safety officer who is able to pass a physical fitness exam cannot be forced into mandatory retirement. In fact, some research examining accident rates for firefighters shows that younger firefighters are injured more frequently than older workers.[9] Because the 1986 amendments covered only private and state and local government workers, the provision of the 1978 amendments allowing federal law enforcement officers and firefighters to be mandatorily retired remains intact.

In 1990, the ADEA was once again amended to include the Older Workers Benefit Protection Act (OWBPA).[10] This act ensures that older workers are not compelled or pressured into waiving their rights under the ADEA. Specifically, the act states that employees who are eligible for early retirement incentive plans must be provided with complete and accurate information concerning what benefits are available under the plan. If certain conditions of the OWBPA are met, employees may then legally sign waivers of their ADEA rights to sue for age discrimination. The eight conditions that must be met for a waiver to comply with the act are the following:

1. The waiver is part of an agreement that specifically states the worker is waiving his or her ADEA rights and is not merely a general release.
2. The agreement containing the waiver does not disclaim any rights or claims arising after the date of its execution.
3. The worker receives value (such as an extra month of severance) in return for signing the agreement.
4. The worker is advised in writing of the right to consult an attorney of his or her choosing before signing the agreement.
5. The worker is advised in writing of his or her right to consider the agreement for a period of twenty-one days before it is effective.

6. The worker is given at least seven days following the execution of the agreement to revoke it.[11]

The OWBPA prohibits the design and administration of employee benefit plans that contain age-based distinctions or otherwise discriminate against employees over the age of forty. The act specifies that a benefit plan will be found discriminatory unless "the actual amount of payment made or cost incurred on behalf of the older worker" is equal to or greater than that for the younger worker. The employer bears the burden of proving that its plan is not discriminatory.

The act provides some exemptions from its coverage. First, the act specifically exempts "voluntary early retirement incentive plans." It appears from the language of the act, and its legislative history, that to fall within this exemption, incentive plans must truly be voluntary. In short, employers apparently may offer carefully drawn early retirement incentives to some pension-eligible employees, provided that there is a valid basis other than age for incentive eligibility (e.g., years of service).

Second, the act specifically exempts employee benefit plan features that work to the advantage of older workers: (1) minimum-age eligibility requirements and (2) subsidized early retirement benefits and Social Security supplements (within certain limits). Third, the OWBPA permits employers to limit the amount of severance pay that is due to terminated pension-eligible employees. Specifically, the legislation provides that employers may deduct the value of any retiree health benefits and additional pension benefits from the amount an employee would otherwise receive as severance pay.[12] There are, however, specific restrictions on these deductions that limit the funds considered severance pay, cap the amount of retiree health benefits that may be included in a severance pay reduction, and mandate the mix of health benefits and additional pension benefits considered in a severance pay reduction.

It should also be noted that when group layoffs or exit incentive programs are involved, the employee must be given

- information on the class of employees covered
- eligibility factors
- time limits applicable
- information as to job titles and ages of individuals eligible or selected
- ages of individuals in same job classification or unit not selected

The courts have strictly held employers to the federal statutory requirements under the OWBPA with respect to employees waiving their rights to sue employers under the ADEA. In *Oubre v. Entergy Operations Inc.* (1998),[13] Dolores Oubre, as part of a termination agreement, signed a release of all claims against her employer Entergy, a power plant in Louisiana, under the ADEA. As part of the agreement, she began receiving severance pay in installments. When the legality of the release came into question, Oubre filed suit against Entergy. The U.S. Supreme Court ruled in this case that the release did not comply with the requirements for a release under the OWBPA in at least the following three respects: (1) the employer did not give the employee enough time to consider her options, (2) the employer did not give the employee seven days after she signed the release to change her mind, and (3) the release made no specific reference to claims under the ADEA. Even though Oubre had begun receiving her financial settlement, and no provisions had been made for her to return the monies to her employer, the Court ruled for Oubre.

One of the most recent developments around the ADEA as of this writing is the U.S. Supreme Court's 2000 decision in *Kimel v. Florida Board of Regents*, which widely reduced the scope of the law.[14] In *Kimel*, the Court barred state employees from suing their employers (i.e., state governments) in federal court to redress age discrimination under the ADEA. The Court ruled that the Fourteenth Amendment's section 5 does not permit Congress to abrogate states' Eleventh Amendment immunity for violations under the ADEA. Unless a state is willing to waive its sovereign immunity, state employees cannot bring a private cause of action for discrimination under the ADEA. In effect, state employees do not have the same age discrimination protections as private sector and federal government employees.[15]

The issue of age discrimination will continue to grow as baby boomers age and older workers remain in the workforce longer. Although age discrimination is prohibited by law, public employers will need to ensure that the law is *enforced* in their workplaces. That is, they will need to take steps to ensure that their workplace is discrimination free, so that the rights of older workers are not abridged under the law. But more than this, older workers will be a viable part of tomorrow's workforces, and so employers must ensure that the needs and interests of older workers are accommodated. This certainly means *not* setting age as a bona fide occupational qualification (BFOQ).

Age as a Bona Fide Occupational Qualification. A bona fide occupational qualification enables an employer to "legally discriminate" on the basis of a particular characteristic, providing that the particular characteristic is an *essential* requirement of the job. If an employer sets age restrictions on a particular job, the courts will require the employer in a BFOQ defense to demonstrate that the specific age requirement is necessary and legitimate for the job.

Employers have also been able to set age restrictions for particular jobs if they can prove that their use of age in an employment decision is "based on reasonable factors other than age" (RFOA). This defense is used to negate any causal link between the age of an employee and the employment practice affecting that employee. In addition, employers can rely on age in making employment decisions where the decision or policy is necessary to "observe the terms of a bona fide seniority system" or "benefit plan." Thus employers can make decisions relative to an employee's age without incurring the costs of applying benefits programs equally to employees of all ages.[16]

It should be noted that the BFOQ exception to the ADEA has been narrowly construed by the courts. It is in the area of public safety where employers have historically sought to set age as a BFOQ. These efforts, however, have generally been unsuccessful.[17] With the ADEA amendments prohibiting mandatory retirement for state and local public safety officers, such cases have become increasingly rare.

The point to be made here is that in the work world of today, where there is a growing number of older workers, it would be counterproductive for organizations to limit the opportunities of older workers by, for example, setting age as a BFOQ. Older workers bring a number of resources to an organization, including institutional history, long-range perspective, expertise, experience, a strong work ethic, dedication, and commitment. Thus restricting their opportunities through BFOQs would not be a sound management practice.

Training and Development

Work environments have undergone significant changes in recent years, thereby requiring the constant adaptation of employees to tools and technologies, and vice versa. In effect, the demand for training and developing government employees has increased substantially. Although governments at every level are faced with shrinking budgets, training programs are critical for ensuring that all workers have the skills and abilities necessary to perform the work of today. In fact, training programs aimed at retaining older workers could be extremely cost-effective in greatly offsetting the costs associated with the loss of expertise and the costs of hiring and training new workers.

One key requirement in general is management support. Providing effective support to all workers in a highly age-diverse workplace can promote an environment that is free of stress and anxiety. It is also essential to *orient* workers about coming changes in the work environment. This will not only reduce potential resistance to change by all employees but will also allow workers to have some input into the changes and possible implications or ramifications of the change. Worker participation may ultimately promote a sense of personal investment in the implementation and outcome of workplace changes. In the context of training for the intergenerational workplace, several areas, as indicated below, could be targeted.

Training and Development in Technology. Today's workforce is composed of a wide range of workers from those who can be referred to as "techy geeks" to those who have never even turned on a computer. The veterans, those classified earlier as persons born prior to World War II, represent a cohort of workers who perhaps never learned about computers, either at work or school. The workplace is a dynamic one, where jobs continue to change and evolve with technology; as a corollary the skills and job requirements will necessarily change. The jobs of yesterday never required the veterans to master computer technology and so, today, the prospect of having to rely on computers can be both intimidating and daunting.

Notwithstanding, it is critical that organizations avoid stereotyping veterans as technophobes. The use of such negative stereotypes can only exacerbate tensions and anxieties about learning new skills. Developing programs to train workers to use the new technologies in the workplace is key to managing intergenerational workforces. Once trained, new technologies will become part of veterans' repertoires of skills, just as typewriters and other mechanical tools did when such technologies were state of the art. And we must not overlook the fact that it was this cohort who invented telephonic and electromechanical concept structures from which were spawned today's highly advanced technologies.[18]

TABLE 6.5   Commonly Held Stereotypes Around Age

Younger employees	Wet behind the ears; know nothing; no respect for traditions; lack experience, therefore have no credibility; not loyal; can't be trusted with responsibility
Older employees	Less motivated to work hard; deadwood; "old farts"; resist change; can't learn new methods; plateaued after 40; buried after 50; "fire" proof

Source: Adapted from Marilyn Loden and Judy B. Rosener *Workforce America!* Homewood, Ill.: Business One Irwin (1991).

Organization theorists suggest that older workers learn best when they are allowed to learn with their age peers, when they can learn at their own pace, when the training is based on respect, and when it minimizes anxieties. Anxiety can be reduced by providing the training far in advance of when the new skills are needed, providing a respectful and supportive learning environment, allowing persons in the same age cohorts to learn together, and offering additional training or educational opportunities for those who desire them.[19] In short, carefully designed and implemented training programs can mitigate any potential disruptions caused by the introduction of new technologies to workforces that are diverse in terms of age.

Training to Combat Negative Stereotypes. Multigenerational workforces require that all employees, supervisors, and managers be trained to dispel negative stereotypes around age. Table 6.5 provides a list of commonly held stereotypes surrounding age. As the table indicates, younger as well as older workers can possess negative stereotypes. These views and attitudes perpetuate negative myths that can only disrupt unity and trust in the workplace. Training programs can help alleviate the detrimental strain associated with negative stereotypes and myths about age (also see Table 6.6).

Flexible Work Arrangements

As noted earlier, retaining older workers will be an important part of diversity programs in the coming years. Older workers bring commitment, strong loyalties, experience, and expertise to organizations.

TABLE 6.6   Fact Versus Fiction Regarding Older Workers

Myth	Fact
They get sick more often and have more accidents.	Older workers have fewer on-the-job accidents, and insurance claims by older workers are no different than those for other employees.
They are not as productive as younger employees.	The U.S. Department of Health and Human Services reports that older workers are just as productive as younger workers.
They are not as bright as younger employees.	The American Management Association reports that psychologists find that intelligence remains constant until at least the age of 70.
They don't want to work.	Many retirees report that they would prefer to be working, at least part-time.
They can't learn new technologies.	Older workers are very willing students, when the training is done properly (e.g., with low stress and respectfully).

Source: Ron Zemke, Claire Raines, and Bob Filipczak, *Generations at Work* (New York: American Management Association, 2000).

Because older workers may desire to extend their work lives for such reasons as work ethic, lifestyle, or financial necessity, developing ways to retain older workers is a prudent business or management practice. Developing flexible work arrangements such as the following is one such strategy:

Part-Time Work.   One way to encourage valuable older workers to remain on the job is to provide part-time opportunities to workers who wish to reduce their hours of work. Because research shows that many older workers would continue working if they could reduce their hours, this is a viable way to retain older workers who might otherwise retire.

Flextime.   Flextime was discussed in Chapter 5 as a way to provide employees with flexible or compressed work schedules. It allows workers to accommodate their needs and family interests by adjusting the traditional fixed schedule of working eight hours a day, five days a week. As noted, an employee could work from 10:00 A.M. to 6:00 P.M., instead of the traditional nine-to-five schedule. Such programs will not only give older workers some control over their work lives but can also improve their productivity.

Flexiplace. Flexiplace, also discussed in Chapter 5, enables employees to perform their jobs at a work site away from the primary office. Such an arrangement would allow older workers to perform their work at home, for example, or at a satellite office and communicate with their offices via telephone or computer. As noted in Chapter 5, the Federal Flexible Workplace Program was established for the purpose of allowing federal employees to work away from the office under such programs as telecommuting.[20] Although we traditionally think of these efforts as a way to accommodate the needs of working women with families, flexiplace options could also motivate valuable older workers to remain on the job longer.

Job Transfers. Many older public employees retire from their government jobs and then do consulting or work in the private sector. Developing job opportunities for lateral transfers into other jobs could serve as an incentive for older workers to stay on the job. Older workers may be retiring because they have plateaued on their jobs and are attempting to find more exciting, stimulating work elsewhere. To the extent this is the case, this option could prove very effective in retaining older workers.

Economic Incentive Programs. Most pension regulations penalize older workers who utilize flexible work arrangements with the same employer. However, some pubic employers are modifying their regulations through legislative change so that older workers would not incur financial loss by remaining on the job. For example, changes to the Kansas Public Employees Retirement System now allow government employees to retire at the age of sixty or later, draw their pensions, and be rehired into their former jobs or other comparable jobs.[21] Creative actions such as this enable government employers to keep valued older workers.

It is important to note that with any of these alternative work arrangements, it would be wise to offer preretirement planning seminars to assist older workers in becoming more knowledgeable about how alternative work options to extend their work lives would impact on their retirement benefits. Although older workers may be very interested in remaining on the job, they would not do so if it represented a financial loss. This makes the need for economic incentives, as noted above, all the more critical.

At the same time, of course, government organizations, as part of their overall strategic planning efforts, must prepare for the fact that senior-level workers will at some point retire, thereby creating a "brain drain." The federal government relies in part on succession planning to help federal agencies identify and develop potential candidates to replace retiring Senior Executive Service (SES) members, those at the highest career posts available to federal workers.[22] Because of their senior level, members of the SES are critical to the execution of agency policy and mission and to the effective management of federal programs. Although a majority of recently surveyed SESers said that their agencies do not have a formal succession planning program for the SES,[23] the government views it as an important strategic process for forecasting and meeting executive resource needs, and it encourages federal agencies to engage in this form of human resources planning.

Motivational Programs

To the extent that older public employees are plateauing in their jobs (i.e., reaching the highest level of promotability), managers will need to develop ways to motivate older workers. Some solutions to this are creating employee–management improvement committees, creating mentoring opportunities, and relying on ad hoc work teams to provide leadership opportunities.[24]

There are two initiatives in the federal government that have been developed to address the problem of plateaued employees. At the NASA Ames Research Center, for example, the Interactive Development for Engineers (IDEAS) program was developed, which allows older workers to meet informally with other employees five times a year for communication and team-building training. The U.S. Department of Labor has developed a two-day seminar intended to assist employees in identifying factors that may contribute to their job satisfaction and ultimately to their overall productivity.[25]

Cafeteria-Style Benefits

As discussed in Chapter 5, cafeteria-style benefit programs allow all employees to select benefits from a menu of choices to best meet their own particular interests. Because older workers' needs may vary from younger workers', and vice versa, this type of approach could effectively respond to *all* employees' benefit needs. For example, older workers may desire better retirement benefit packages, while younger workers may prefer more leave opportunities. The important point is that the needs of an intergenerational workforce may differ substantially, and cafeteria-style benefit programs may be one approach to address this issue.

Conclusion

As government employers develop diversity programs to better manage workforces of the twenty-first century, age is an important characteristic that should not be overlooked. As the workplace continues to become increasingly intergenerational, strategies to harness the resources of individuals at all ages can help build a stable, harmonious, and ultimately productive workforce.

Notes

1. *Workforce 2020* (Indianapolis: Hudson Institute, 1997), p. 5.

2. Ibid., p. 94.

3. Ron Zemke, Claire Raines, and Bob Filipczak, *Generations at Work* (New York: American Management Association, 2000).

4. The U.S. General Accounting Office estimates that by 2004, nearly 30 percent of federal employees will be eligible to retire, with another 19 percent eligible for early retirement. Despite eligibility, however, it may be the case that federal workers are choosing to work longer.

5. See Zemke, Raines, and Filipczak, *Generations*.

6. Ibid.

7. As Levin-Epstein notes, the ADEA was extended to federal workers under 1974 amendments to the Fair Labor Standards Act. See Michael Levin-Epstein, *Primer of Equal Employment Opportunity*, 4th ed. (Washington, D.C.: Bureau of National Affairs, 1987), p. 83.

8. This aspect of the law mandated retirement for law enforcement officers and firefighters who reached age fifty-five and had completed twenty years of service. See Eric Andrew Fox, "Note: An Examination of Mandatory Retirement Provisions for Police Officers," *Suffolk Journal of Trial and Appellate Advocacy* 5 (2000).

9. This may be due, however, to the fact that older workers have moved into supervisory roles over the span of their careers and therefore are not exposed to the same risks on the job. See, for example, Joan E. Pynes, "The ADEA and Its Exemptions on the Mandatory Retirement Provisions for Firefighters," *Review of Public Personnel Administration* 15 (1995): 34–45.

10. The OWBPA is not to be confused with the broad-based Older Americans Act (AoA) of 1965. As amended, the AoA is designed to help seniors lead healthy, independent lives. Some of its provisions include improving and simplifying services such as Meals on Wheels, targeting resources to seniors who are the most needy, protecting senior citizen programs from abuse, fraud, and waste, and improving employment opportunities for low-income seniors.

11. See http://www.ahipubs.com/FAQ/benefits/older.html.

12. See http://www.seyfarth.com/practice/labor/articles/ll_1031.html.

13. *Oubre v. Entergy Operations Inc.*, 522 U.S. 422 (1998).

14. *Kimel v. Florida Board of Regents*, 528 U.S. 62 (2000).

15. As of this writing, a bill is being proposed that will counteract the Court's *Kimel* decision, thereby restoring the rights of state employees to sue in age discrimination cases.

16. The U.S. Supreme Court first outlined a two-pronged test for what constitutes a BFOQ in *Western Air Lines, Inc. v. Criswell*, 472 U.S. 400 (1985). The *Criswell* Court adopted this test from the U.S. Court of Appeals for the Fifth Circuit ruling in *Usery V. Tamiami Trail Tours*, 531 F.2d 224 (5th Cir. 1976).

17. See, for example, *Johnson v. Mayor of Baltimore*, 472 U.S. 353 (1985), where the U.S. Supreme Court struck down the city of Baltimore's policy of retiring firefighters at age fifty-five.

18. Zemke, Raines, and Filipczak, *Generations.*

19. See, for example, Dale E. Yeatts, W. Edward Folts, and James Knapp, "Older Workers' Adaptation to a Changing Workplace," *Educational Gerontology* 26 (2000): 565–573.

20. Also see Chapter 5, where it was noted that the federal government is challenged to increase telecommuting opportunities for federal employees given that they find it an attractive work arrangement. See MSPB, "Issues of Merit," *MSPB Newsletter*, December 2000.

21. See George Henderson, *Cultural Diversity in the Workplace* (Westport, Conn.: Quorum, 1994).

22. See U.S. General Accounting Office, *Senior Executive Service: Retirement Trends Underscore the Importance of Succession Planning* (Washington, D.C., 2000). It should be noted that this report provides an analysis of six thousand SESers. The findings indicate that the rate at which career SESers retire varies widely, from a low of 2 percent in 1992 to a high of 10 percent in 1994 (see p. 21).

23. Ibid., p. 30.

24. See Robert H. Elliott, "Human Resource Management's Role in the Future Aging of the Workforce," *Review of Public Personnel Administration* 15 (1995): 15–17.

25. Ibid.

Additional Reading

American Outlook. "Special Section: The Graying of America." Fall 1998, pp. 28–50. Published by the Hudson Institute, Indianapolis.

Cayer, N. Joseph. *Public Personnel Administration in the United States*. 3d ed. New York: St. Martin's, 1996.

Czaja, S. J., and J. Sharit. "Age Difference in the Performance of Computer-Based Work: A Function of Pacing and Task Complexity." *Psychology and Aging* 8 (1993): 59–67.

Elliot, Robert H. "Human Resources Management's Role in the Future Aging of the Workforce." *Review of Public Personnel Administration*, Spring 1995. Symposium.

Griffiths, Amanda. "Work Design and Management: The Older Worker." *Experimental Aging Research* 25 (1999): 411–421.

Herz, D. E., and P. L. Rone. "Institutional Barriers to Employment of Older Workers." *Monthly Labor Review*, April 1989, pp. 14–21.

Jurkiewicz, Carole L., and Roger G. Brown. "GenXers v. Boomers vs. Matures." *Review of Public Personnel Administration* 18 (1995): 18–37.

Klingner, Donald E., and John Nalbandian. *Public Personnel Management: Contexts and Strategies*. 4th ed. Englewood Cliffs, N.J.: Prentice-Hall, 1998.

Marshall, Victor W. "Reasoning with Case Studies: Issues of an Aging Workforce." *Journal of Aging Studies* 13 (1999): 377–390.

Miller, C. S., J. A. Kaspin, and M. H. Schuster. "The Impact of Performance Appraisal Methods on Age Discrimination in Employment Cases." *Personnel Psychology* 43 (1990): 555–578.

Pynes, Joan E. "The ADEA and Its Exemptions on the Mandatory Retirement Provisions for Firefighters." *Review of Public Personnel Administration* 15 (1995): 34–45.

Rix, Sara. "The Challenge of an Aging Work Force: Keeping Older Workers Employed and Employable." *Journal of Aging and Social Policy* 8 (1996): 79–98.

Roberts, Gary E. "Age-Related Employment Issues in Florida Municipal Governments." *Review of Public Personnel Administration* 15 (1995): 62–83.

Schwoerer, Catherine E., and Douglas R. May. "Age and Work Outcomes: The Moderating Effects of Self-efficacy and Tool Design Effectiveness." *Journal of Organizational Behavior* 17 (1996): 469–488.

Shepard, Roy J. "Age and Physical Work Capacity." *Experimental Aging Research* 25 (1999): 331–343.

U.S. General Accounting Office. *Federal Retirement: Federal and Private Sector Retirement Program Benefits Vary*. Washington, D.C., April 1997.

_____. *Federal Retirement: Key Elements Are Included in Agencies' Education Programs*. Washington, D.C., March 1999.

Walker, Alan. "Combating Age Discrimination at the Workplace." *Experimental Aging Research* 25 (1999): 367–378.

7

Diversity in Ability

As discussed throughout this book, the technological advances of the twenty-first century have brought new jobs and, as a corollary, new job opportunities to the American workplace. Many workers have benefited from the resulting employment prosperity. However, another segment of the American workforce has been completely closed out of these opportunities—for no other reason than the different ways in which these workers approach and perform the job tasks and functions. The cornerstone of this book rests on the notion or concept of differences. One difference that must be considered in the realm of managing workplace diversity programs is difference in abilities.

The U.S. Census Bureau has estimated that nearly one-fifth of all Americans have some type of disability, and about one in ten have a severe disability (i.e., someone who uses an assistive device to get around, such as a wheelchair, or needs assistance from another person to perform basic activities). The Census Bureau also anticipates that, given the aging of the population and the increased likelihood of having a disability as one ages, the growth in the number of people with disabilities will increase greatly as we move into the twenty-first century.[1]

This chapter examines managing a workplace with workers of all abilities. It begins by looking at workforce demographics in the federal government. It then explores the various strategies for ensuring that all workers, regardless of ability, are fully integrated into the organizational community that is ultimately responsible for meeting the needs and interests of the American public.

TABLE 7.1   Executive Branch (Nonpostal) Employment, by Disability
Status and Disabled Veterans, 1986–1998

	1986	1988	1990	1992	1996	1998
Total	2,083,985	2,125,148	2,150,359	2,175,715	1,890,406	1,804,591
Disability						
Disabled	128,123	132,317	140,169	153,197	132,344	124,139
% Disabled	6.6	6.6	6.9	7.4	7.3	7.1
Not identified	154,332	131,751	112,347	98,662	70,989	63,175
% Not identified	7.4	6.2	5.2	4.5	3.8	3.5
Disabled veterans						
All disabled veterans	91,797	90,087	89,918	90,752	82,480	80,973
% all veterans	12.6	13.2	14.0	14.8	16.3	17.3

Source: U.S. Office of Personnel Management (OPM), www.opm.gov.

The Differently Abled Workplace

Table 7.1 presents data on persons with disabilities, including veterans, in the federal workforce. As the data show, there was almost a steady representation of disabled persons in the federal government from 1986 to 1998. For disabled veterans, however, the data show that there was an increase for the same time period.

Tables 7.2 and 7.3 show additional information on the representation of disabled persons in the federal government workforce. Table 7.2 shows that for white-collar workers, the highest concentration of disabled persons is found in clerical positions, followed by technical positions. The data also show a relatively high percentage of disabled workers (8.53) in blue-collar jobs in the federal workplace. Table 7.3 shows a further breakdown by executive branch agency. Interestingly, the highest concentration of disabled persons occurs in the State Department, with 13.9 percent. One might have expected to find the highest concentration in either Veterans Affairs or Health and Human Services.

TABLE 7.2   Disability Status within Federal Government Occupational Category, 1998

Occupational Category	Total Respondents	Disabled Persons (percentages)
All Categories	1,741,416	7.13
White-Collar Total	1,506,926	6.91
Professional	423,386	5.05
Administrative	507,153	6.37
Technical	336,606	8.25
Clerical	193,074	10.86
Other	46,707	3.65
Blue-Collar Total	234,490	8.53

Source: U.S. Office of Personnel Management (OPM), www.opm.gov.

Strategies for Managing Diversity in Ability

A comprehensive program for managing diversity in public sector workforces must obviously include a component addressing disabled persons. Perhaps one of the critical aspects of diversity programs as they pertain to disabled persons is conducting "needs assessments." Public and private sector employers alike are finding that surveying disabled persons around their needs is an important first step in ensuring that the workplace meets and accommodates their needs, concerns, and interests.

Eradicating Discrimination in the Workplace

There are a number of laws prohibiting employment discrimination on the basis of a disability. One of the earliest laws was the Vocational Rehabilitation Act of 1973 as amended, which prohibits discrimination against qualified disabled persons. In 1990, protections against employment discrimination were strengthened by Title I of the Americans with Disabilities Act (ADA).[2] The ADA covers non–federal government em-

TABLE 7.3   Disabled Employees in Federal Government, by Agency, 1998 (Percentages)

Agency	Total Disabled Persons
Total Executive Branch	7.1
Executive Office of the President	2.1
Agriculture	7.8
Commerce	6.0
Defense	7.7
Energy	6.1
Health & Human Services	6.2
Housing & Urban Development	9.3
Interior	5.4
Justice	3.2
Labor	6.9
State	13.9
Transportation	4.9
Treasury	6.9
Veterans Affairs	8.6

Source: U.S. Office of Personnel Management (OPM), www.opm.gov.

ployers, employment agencies, labor unions, and joint labor–management committees with fifteen or more employees. The federal government, which is excluded from the ADA, continues to be covered by executive orders and the Rehabilitation Act.

Under President Clinton, the federal government took the further step of making a commitment to develop public policy that would provide clear direction to both the public and private sectors on employing persons with disabilities. To this end, President Clinton signed Executive Order 13078 on March 13, 1998, establishing the Presidential Task Force on Employment of Adults with Disabilities. The mission of the task force is to create a coordinated, aggressive national policy to bring adults with disabilities into gainful employment at a rate as close as possible to that of the general adult population.

Both the Rehabilitation Act and the ADA state that an individual can claim to be disabled if she or he

1. has a physical or mental impairment that substantially limits one or more of the major life activities of the individual
2. has a record of having such an impairment
3. is regarded as having such an impairment

Physical impairments include anatomical losses, cancer, deformities, HIV/AIDS, heart disease, impairments that affect speech, hearing, and sight. To date, there has been no definitive ruling as to the disabled status of obese individuals.[3] Mental impairments include mental retardation, mental illness, and others.

In addition to its antidiscrimination component, the Vocational Rehabilitation Act requires the federal government and federal contractors with contracts in excess of $2,500 to take affirmative action in hiring, placing, and advancing disabled persons. The ADA, however, does not incorporate affirmative action requirements. It is also important to note that the ADA protects "qualified" individuals with a disability. Thus a disabled person who can perform essential job functions, with or without reasonable accommodation, is considered qualified for the job (see Table 7.4). It is illegal to consider a worker unqualified because of the person's inability to perform marginal or incidental job functions.

Eradicating discrimination against disabled persons is a critical first step in successfully managing diversity in the workplace. An important second step is providing reasonable accommodations for disabled persons. Indeed, reasonable accommodations are mandated under the ADA. Reasonable accommodations refer to any modification or adjustment to a job or work environment that will enable the worker with a disability to perform the job. Such accommodations include, for example, constructing wheelchair ramps, offering flextime, providing special assistants (e.g., readers or interpreters), and acquiring or modifying workplace equipment. An employer is not required to made an accommodation if it would impose an "undue hardship" on the employer. Undue hardship is defined as "an action requiring significant difficulty or expense."[4]

TABLE 7.4 Frequently Asked Questions under the ADA

Question	Answer
May an employer inquire as to whether a prospective employee is disabled?	No. An employer may not make a preemployment inquiry on an application form or in an interview as to whether, or to what extent, an individual is disabled. The employer may, however, ask a job applicant if she or he can perform particular job functions.
Can an employer refuse to hire an applicant or fire a current employee who is illegally using drugs?	Yes. Individuals who currently engage in the illegal use of drugs are specifically excluded from the definition of "qualified individual with a disability" protected by the ADA when an action is taken on the basis of their drug use.
Are applicants or employees who are currently illegally using drugs covered by the ADA?	No. Individuals who currently engage in the illegal use of drugs are specifically excluded from the definition of "qualified individual with a disability" protected by the ADA when the employer takes action on the basis of their drug use.
Are alcoholics covered by the ADA?	Yes. Although a current illegal user of drugs is not protected by the ADA if an employer acts on the basis of such use, a person who currently uses alcohol is not automatically denied protection. An alcoholic is a person with a disability and is protected by the ADA if she or he is qualified to perform the essential functions of the job. An employer may be required to provide an accommodation to an alcoholic.
Does the ADA mandate affirmative action?	No. But it also *does not* preclude an employer from taking affirmative steps to hiring disabled persons.
Who is a "qualified individual with a disability"?	A qualified individual with a disability is a person who meets legitimate skill, experience, education, or other requirements of an employment position that s/he holds or seeks, and who can perform the essential functions of the position with or without reasonable accommodation.

TABLE 7.4   *(continued)*

Question	Answer
Does the ADA override federal and state health and safety laws?	The ADA does not override health and safety requirements established under other federal laws even if a standard adversely affects the employment of an individual with disability. If a standard is required by another federal law, an employer must comply with it and does not have to show that the standard is job related and consistent with business necessity.
How are the employment provisions enforced?	The employment provisions of the ADA are enforced under the same procedures applicable to race, color, gender, national origin, and religious discrimination under Title VII of the Civil Rights Act of 1964, as amended, and the Civil Rights Act of 1991. Complaints regarding actions that occurred on or after July 26, 1992, may be filed with the Equal Employment Opportunity Commission or designated state human rights agencies.

Source: Adapted from U.S. Equal Employment Opportunity Commission and U.S. Department of Justice Civil Rights Division, Americans with Disabilities Act, "Questions and Answers," http://www.usdoj.gov/crt/ada/qandaeng.htm.

The ADA has resulted in a surprisingly small number of lawsuits—only about 650 nationwide in five years. This is small, given that there are over 6 million businesses in the United States, 666,000 public and private employers, and eighty thousand units of state and local government that must comply with the ADA.[5] One of the most recent and significant U.S. Supreme Court cases around the ADA is *Sutton v. United Air Lines* (1999).[6] In this case, twin sisters Sutton and Hinton, who suffer from myopia, filed suit against United Air Lines under the ADA when they were denied employment for the position of airline pilot. Sutton and Hinton have uncorrected visual acuity of 20/200 or worse, but with corrective measures, both function identically to individuals without similar impairments. The airline rejected their bid for employment because they did not meet United's minimum requirement of uncorrected visual acuity of 20/100 or better.

The U.S. District Court dismissed the sisters' complaint and held that petitioners were not actually disabled under subsection (A) of the ADA disability definition because they could fully correct their visual impairments. The U.S. Court of Appeals for the Tenth Circuit affirmed. The decision was then upheld by the U.S. Supreme Court, which stated that the severely myopic sisters, Sutton and Hinton, "were not disabled within the meaning of ADA, because applicants could fully correct their visual impairment with corrective lenses."[7]

The one area surrounding the ADA where there continues to be some court activity is HIV/AIDS. As noted, unlike the Rehabilitation Act, the ADA protects persons who have Acquired Immunodeficiency Syndrome (AIDS) or the retrovirus, Human Immunodeficiency Virus (HIV), that causes AIDS. Early on, this particular disability generated a good deal of concern, indeed, hysteria in the workplace. People were afraid to drink from the same water fountains as persons suspected of having HIV or AIDS, use the same bathrooms, or touch the same doorknobs. Employers gradually responded with policies to protect persons with HIV/AIDS (e.g., around discrimination, privacy, and confidentiality). Despite enhanced knowledge about the causes of the disease, people continue to react negatively to coworkers or clients suspected of being infected. And, notwithstanding the ADA, discrimination in the workplace and in social settings prevails. Thus government employers are further challenged to develop stronger protections and reasonable accommodations for persons with HIV/AIDS.

Although employees with HIV/AIDS have sought relief under the ADA, they have largely not prevailed in their claims. Generally, plaintiffs have encountered difficulties in even getting their cases heard by a jury because employers have been effective in having claims dismissed prior to trial.[8] However, the recent U.S. Supreme Court judgment in *Bragdon v. Abbott* (1998),[9] although not an employment case, may lead to more successful legal challenges by employees with HIV/AIDS.[10] In *Bragdon*, Ms. Abbott successfully sued her dentist, who refused to fill a cavity because she was infected with the HIV virus. The *Bragdon* Court ruled that Abbott did have an ADA-covered disability because Abbott was substantially limited in the major life activity of reproduction. Importantly, the Court further held that *asymptomatic* HIV infection is a disability under the ADA, thus clarifying a battle between lower courts over the issue of whether HIV must be symptomatic or asymptomatic in order to be considered a disability under the ADA.[11] The Court's ruling in *Bragdon* has been interpreted by many as a critical development of law under the employment section, Title I, of the ADA.[12]

One of the most recent legal developments around the ADA as of this writing is an Eleventh Amendment challenge to the law. Similar to the circumstances surrounding the U.S. Supreme Court's ruling in *Kimel v. Florida Board of Regents*,[13] as discussed in Chapter 6 around age discrimination, the state of Alabama has asserted that it is immune from ADA suits[14] under the Eleventh Amendment of the U.S. Constitution. The Supreme Court interprets the Eleventh Amendment to bar private lawsuits for damages in federal court against a state that has not given its consent to be sued, unless Congress has validly abrogated a state's immunity. The U.S. Court of Appeals for the Eleventh Circuit in *Garrett v. the University of Alabama* (1999),[15] in overturning the federal district court decision, ruled that the ADA is not only valid but is also a legitimate use of congressional authority; thus the court rejected Alabama's immunity claim.[16]

In February 2001, however, the U.S. Supreme Court overturned the appellate court decision. Consistent with a series of decisions over the past several years, the Court restricted the scope of Title I of the ADA and at the same time strengthened state sovereignty. The Court first ruled that Congress should have made its intentions about the scope of the ADA clear in the record or text of the legislation. The Court majority then went on to say that in order to make states liable to private suits for damages, it was inappropriate for Congress to consider general societal discrimination against people with disabilities. Rather, the Court went on to say, Congress must demonstrate a high level of proof that the states themselves had engaged in unconstitutional discrimination.[17]

In practical terms, the Garrett decision resulted in nearly 5 million state workers losing their federal protection from disability discrimination. Although the decisions continue to allow state workers to sue state governments, they can do so only in state court, and then only if the state agrees to the suit. Moreover, the suit must be brought under state disability laws, which are often weaker, less effective, and narrower in scope (e.g., in terms of reasonable accommodations) than the ADA. In the end, the ADA, like other laws, has fallen victim to a power struggle between the legislative and judicial branches of government, thus leaving those intended to be served by the law disadvantaged, to say the least.

Training and Development

Disabled workers are just like any other workers who may need training in order to perform the required tasks and functions associated with a

TABLE 7.5   Commonly Held Physical Ability Stereotypes

Differently Abled	Physical impairment equals intellectual impairment; charity cases, fortunate to have jobs; should be pitied; can't carry own load; have no romantic/sexual/emotional life; success is qualified ("not bad for a handicapped person")
Physically Able-Bodied	Assume all disabilities can be seen and recognized; patronizing; deny own frailty/morality; amazed at accomplishments of differently abled; overreact

Source: Adapted from Marilyn Loden and Judy B. Rosener *Workforce America!* Homewood, Ill.: Business One Irwin (1991).

particular job. Interfacing disabled workers with the technology that may be needed for reasonable accommodation purposes may also be necessary. For example, if a voice-activated computer and voice-recognition software are purchased for a seeing-impaired worker, some training will be in order to ensure that the worker can properly use the equipment. As one expert on workers with disabilities points out, the more effective organizations "integrate workers with disabilities into a competitive work setting, while providing continuous support services for them."[18] Training for coworkers also facilitates the integration of disabled workers in the workplace, especially in terms of dispelling negative stereotypes, as seen in the following section.

Training to Combat Negative Stereotypes.   Training is needed to educate workers as well as supervisors about the myths and stereotypes surrounding physical and mental abilities (see Table 7.5). Perhaps one of the greatest fallacies is that disabled persons take more time off than persons without disabilities. Table 7.6 shows that this is not the case. In fact, there are only relatively minor differences in the overall work patterns between workers with disabilities and those with no disabilities: disability status made very little difference to the proportion of workers who worked the entire month.

A study conducted by Cornell University in March 2000 found that the most significant and difficult barrier faced by disabled workers in the workplace is bias by nondisabled workers.[19] The survey further found that government and private sector employers alike believe that lack of training and related work experience have hampered their disabled staff. The survey also indicated that private employers often lag behind feder-

TABLE 7.6   Work Patterns of Employed persons 20–64 Years of Age, by Disability Status and Industry, 1994

	Persons with No Disability % who worked		With Moderate Disability % who worked		With severe disability % who worked	
	Entire Month	Full Time	Entire Month	Full Time	Entire Month	Full Time
Agriculture	97.8	86.0	85.7	81.2	90.0	71.7
Nonagricultural	96.8	85.3	94.0	80.5	91.3	66.2
Government	98.1	86.3	95.8	83.6	92.5	70.6

Source: Adapted from Thomas W. Hale, Howard V. Hayghe, and John M. McNeil, "Persons with Disabilities: Labor Market Activity, 1994," *Monthly Labor Review*, September 1998, pp. 3–12.

al ones in aiding disabled workers. For example, 90 percent of government employers reported having acquired or altered equipment to assist disabled employees, but only 59 percent of private employers had done so. On the other hand, the survey found that attitudes and stereotypes are a greater barrier for disabled in federal as compared with private sector workplaces (43 percent to 22 percent).

It is critical to train and educate workers about the nature of mental disabilities. For example, the ADA includes learning disabilities as a mental impairment, and this type of disability can lead to major struggles for the employees, not only in terms of their own work performance but also in terms of negative reactions from coworkers. Employers are challenged not only to make reasonable accommodations for persons with mental impairments but also to increase the sensitivity of all workers toward such disabilities.

As noted earlier, persons with HIV/AIDS continue to face obstacles in the workplace because of myths and ignorance around what causes the disease. Employers are challenged to train and educate workers on the facts about the spread of HIV/AIDS and its causes. This could dispel groundless fears among workers and ultimately lead to greater harmony and productivity in the workplace.

In sum, training and educating workers to address their fears and negative stereotypes of disabled workers is an important component to employers' overall diversity efforts.

Promotion Opportunities

A good deal of research shows that although disabled workers are making some inroads into public employment, they continue to be concentrated in lower-level, lower-paying jobs that carry no policymaking responsibilities.[20] As reported in Table 7.2, disabled persons are more likely to be found in clerical positions in the federal government as opposed to professional and administrative positions. To the extent that government employers are serious about their diversity programs, they will need to provide training and promotion opportunities to disabled employees so that they can advance in government employment. Necessary support services should be available so that advancement opportunities for disabled workers are both fair and realistic.

Flexible Work Arrangements

Many of the flexible work programs discussed in Chapters 5–6 would be important and applicable to disabled persons in the workplace and would also fulfill requirements for reasonable accommodations. For example, part-time work represents one way to accommodate the needs of disabled workers, at least for those who desire a reduced workweek. Another viable option is flextime, which enables workers to adjust the traditional nine-to-five workweek to better serve their particular needs. Flexiplace, also discussed in greater detail in Chapters 5–6, is another flexible work program that allows workers to perform their jobs away from the primary work site. Under such an arrangement, workers could perform their job functions at home or at a satellite office, relying on telecommunications to stay connected with the primary office. These types of flexible work programs not only provide disabled workers some control over their work lives but can lead to greater job satisfaction and ultimately higher productivity.

Employee Benefit Programs

There is a common belief that workers with disabilities consume more health care benefits and therefore drive up the overall costs of health care. Although there is no empirical evidence to support this, such a belief can lead to discrimination in the workplace, as employers will not hire disabled workers. It is important to note, however, that it is illegal under the ADA to consider potential use of health benefits.[21]

Many disabled persons have disabilities that are relatively stable (e.g., hearing loss) and do not require medical treatment any different from the medical care required by able-bodied workers.[22] Employers are thus challenged to dispel the misperception that disabled workers will generate higher health care costs.

The ADA and sound public personnel and human resources policy require that disabled persons have equal access to health care benefits. For the disabled, as for all workers, employee benefits are a critical part of an employment package or contract. As discussed elsewhere in this book, as part of overall diversity programs, an increasing number of employers are offering cafeteria-style benefit programs that allow all employees to select benefits from a menu of options in order to better meet their own particular needs. Again, to the extent that employers are serious about effectively managing diversity in their organizations, this type of benefit plan could prove to be extraordinarily viable.

Conclusion

As public employers develop programs to manage diversity in their organizations, they are challenged to include disabled workers. This growing segment of the American workforce represents an untapped organizational resource that can contribute significantly to the overall performance and productivity of government agencies. Greater efforts to manage all workers more effectively can ultimately lead to stronger, more effective governance of American society.

Notes

1. "Disabilities Affect One-Fifth of All Americans," United States Bureau of the Census, *Census Brief*, December 1997.

2. Other titles of the Americans with Disabilities Act cover other forms of discrimination, including access to public accommodations and services.

3. See, for example, Jeffrey Garcia, "Weight-Based Discrimination and the Americans with Disabilities Act: Is There an End in Sight?" *Hofstra Labor Law Journal*, Fall 1995, pp. 209 237. It should further be noted that weight has been upheld as a bona fide occupational qualification (BFOQ) in many jobs, including public safety. Also see *Cook v. Rhode Island*, 10 F.3d 17 (1st Cir. 1993), where the First Circuit Court of Appeals determined that the refusal by the Rhode Island Department of Mental Health, Retardation, and Hospital to hire an individual due solely to the individual's morbid obesity may violate § 504 of the Rehabilitation Act.

4. See http://www.eeoc.gov/laws/ada.html.

5. See http://www.usdoj.gov/crt/ada/pubs/mythfct.txt.

6. *Sutton v. United Air Lines*, 527 U.S. 471 (1999).

7. *Sutton v. United Air Lines* (1999) at p. 471.

8. Rex J. Zgarba, "Employee's Panacea or Pandora's Box? An Analysis of Bragdon v. Abbott and Its Likely Effects upon Claims Under Title I of the ADA," *Review of Litigation*, Summer 2000, pp. 719–741.

9. *Bragdon v. Abbott*, 524 U.S. 624 (1998).

10. See, for example, Zgarba, "Employee's Panacea"; and Jonathan R. Mook, "Ruling That HIV Is a Disability Could Open Pandora's Box of ADA Claims," *Employment L. Strategist* 4 (1998): 1–9.

11. See Christiana M. Ajalat, "Is HIV Really a 'Disability'? The Scope of the Americans with Disabilities Act after *Bragdon v. Abbott*, 118 S.Ct. 2196 (1998)." *Harvard Journal of Law and Public Policy*, Spring 1999, pp. 751–770.

12. See, for example, Rex J. Zgarba, "Employee's Panacea"; Mook, "Ruling That HIV Is a Disability."

13. *Kimel v. Florida Board of Regents*, 528 U.S. 62 (2000).

14. The state also claimed immunity under the Rehabilitation Act of 1973 and the Family Medical Leave Act of 1993.

15. *Garrett v. the University of Alabama*, 193 F.3d 1214 (11th Cir. 1999).

16. The *Garrett* Appellate Court also ruled that the state of Alabama was not immune from suits under the Rehabilitation Act but that, under the circumstances before the court in this particular case, it was immune from suit under the Family Medical Leave Act. See *Garrett v. the University of Alabama* (1999) at p. 1214.

17. *Garrett v. the University of Alabama; cert. granted,* 120 S. Ct. 1669 (2000); *Garrett v. the University of Alabama*, 2001 U.S. LEXIS 1700 (February 21, 2001). Also see Linda Greenhouse, "Justices Give the States Immunity from Suits by Disabled Workers," *New York Times*, February 22, 2001, pp. A1, A21.

18. George Henderson, *Cultural Diversity in the Workplace* (Westport, Conn.: Quorum, 1994), p. 107.

19. Susanne Bruyère, *Disability Employment Policies and Practices in Private and Federal Sector Organizations* (Ithaca, N.Y.: Cornell University, School of Industrial and Labor Relations Extension Division, Program on Employment and Disability, 2000).

20. See, for example, Pan· S. Kim, "Disability Policy: An Analysis of the Employment of People with Disabilities in the American Federal Government," *Public Personnel Management*, Spring 1996, pp. 73–88.

21. Anthony Patrick Carnevale and Susan Carol Stone, *The American Mosaic* (New York: McGraw-Hill, 1995).

22. Ibid.

Additional Reading

Byers, Keith Alan. "No One Is Above the Law When It Comes to the ADA and the Rehabilitation Act—Not Even Federal, State, or Local Law Enforcement Agencies." *Loyola of Los Angeles Law Review*, April 1997, pp. 977–1051.

Condrey, Steven E., and Jeffrey Brudney. "The Americans with Disabilities Act of 1990: Assessing Its Implementation in America's Largest Cities." *American Review of Public Administration* 28 (1998): 26–42.

Gilbride, Dennis. "Employers' Attitudes Toward Hiring Persons with Disabilities and Vocational Rehabilitation Services." *Journal of Rehabilitation*, October-December 2000, pp. 17–23.

Johnson, William G., and Marjorie Baldwin. "The Americans with Disabilities Act: Will It Make a Difference?" *Policy Studies Journal* 21 (1993): 775–789.

Keeton, Kato B. "AIDS-Related Attitudes Among Government Employees: Implications for Training Programs." *Review of Public Personnel Administration*, Spring 1993, pp. 65–81.

Keeton, Kato B., and Denise L. Brewton. "A Comparative Analysis of AIDS-Related Attitudes Between Public and Private Sector Employees." *Review of Public Personnel Administration*, Summer 1995, pp. 44–59.

Lee, Robert D., Jr. "The Rehabilitation Act and Federal Employment." *Review of Public Personnel Administration*, Fall 1999, pp. 45–64.

Lee, Robert D., Jr., and Paul Greenlaw. "Rights and Responsibilities of Employees and Employers Under the Americans with Disabilities Act of 1990." *Journal of Individual Employment Rights* 7 (1998–1999): 1–13.

Ravitch, Frank S. "Beyond Reasonable Accommodation: The Availability and Structure of a Cause of Action for Workplace Harassment Under the Americans with Disabilities Act." *Cardozo Law Review*, March 1994, pp. 1475–1522.

Rutman, Irvin D. "How Psychiatric Disability Expresses Itself as a Barrier to Employment." *Psychosocial Rehabilitation Journal*, January 1994, pp. 15–34.

Saideman, Ellen M. "The ADA as a Tool for Advocacy: A Strategy for Fighting Employment Discrimination Against People with Disabilities." *Journal of Law and Health* 8 (1993–1994): 47–87.

Shoup, Jennifer. "Title I: Protecting the Obese Worker?" *Indiana Law Review* 29 (1995): 206–229.

Slack, James D. "The Americans with Disabilities Act and the Workplace: Observations about Management's Responsibilities in AIDS-Related Situations." *Public Administration Review*, July-August, 1995.

Sunoo, Brenda Paik. "EEOC Redefines ADA Definitions." *Personnel Journal*, September 1994, pp. 1, 8.

Tsang, Hector, Paul Lam, Bacon Ng, and Odelia Leung. "Predictors of Employment Outcome for People with Psychiatric Disabilities: A Review of the Literature Since the Mid '80s." *Journal of Rehabilitation*, April-June 2000, pp. 19–32.

Yelin, Edward H. *Disability and the Displaced Worker*. Rutgers, N.J.: Rutgers University Press, 1992.

8

Diversity and Sexual Orientation

As public opinion continues to become more positive around sexual orientation, we may see more and more people "coming out of the closet" on their jobs.[1] Indeed, public acceptance is perhaps the sine qua non in the creation of formal and informal protections for gays and lesbians. When society is more accepting, gays, lesbians, and bisexuals feel more comfortable being themselves, and when the public demands gay rights laws, government enact them.[2] The latter is particularly critical given that currently there are no national laws prohibiting employment discrimination against gays, lesbians, and bisexuals. Thus employers are free to fire someone solely on the basis of sexual orientation. Executive Order 13087 issued in 1998 prohibits discrimination on the basis of sexual orientation in federal employment, and there are similar protections offered by some state and local governments for public employees. But no federal law offers similar protections for public or private sector employees. Although gays, lesbians, and bisexuals are no longer required to disclose their sexual orientation on an application for military service, the "Don't Ask, Don't Tell" policy states that homosexual conduct, including the mere statement that one is a gay male, lesbian, or bisexual, is still grounds for discharge from the military.

As government employers develop policies and programs to manage their diverse workforces, it is critical that sexual orientation not be overlooked. This is an area that, for reasons associated with negative connotations, stigma, fear, and ignorance, has been virtually absent from the language of public personnel policies until recently. Those more progressive public and private sector employers who recognize the importance of creating a hostility-free environment for *all* workers will include sexual orientation as part of their overall diversity efforts. *Advocate* magazine, one of the major national gay and lesbian news magazines in the United

States, named a private sector corporation, IBM, as one of the "25 Top Companies to Work for Now" in 1999 in recognition of its diversity policies toward gays, lesbians, and bisexuals.

This chapter begins with a brief discussion of some of the general obstacles that gays, lesbians, and bisexuals face in our society. With this as a backdrop, it then looks at workplace issues, particularly the various strategies that employers have developed or could develop to manage diversity with respect to sexual orientation. Although sexual orientation is not an evident characteristic, as race and gender may be, employers cannot afford to overlook the fact that their workforces are composed of diverse peoples in every sense.

Background

There is a dearth of research on the employment of gays, lesbians, and bisexuals. For obvious reasons, there are virtually no statistics on the extent to which they are employed in public sector workforces. Norma Carr-Ruffino, a professor of management at San Francisco State University, estimates that about one in every fifty persons in the workplace is gay or lesbian.[3] Although the accuracy of this estimate is uncertain, we do know, as remarked at the beginning of this chapter, that more and more people are coming out in the workplace. This is not to say, of course, that the overall climate for gays, lesbians, and bisexuals does not remain chilly. Indeed, the violent murder of a young gay man, Matthew Shepard, in the fall of 1998 and the U.S. Supreme Court's June 2000 decision allowing the Boy Scouts of America (BSA)[4] to expel an exemplary member because he is gay are merely two incidents that reflect the hatred and homophobia in our society.

Consider the following facts published by the National Gay and Lesbian Task Force (NGLTF), a national organization working for the civil rights of gay, lesbian, bisexual, and transgendered people:

Antimarriage Legislation/Amendments

To date, thirty states have adopted some form of antimarriage legislation and/or amendment. Divisive battles to ban same-sex marriage continue with recent ballot initiatives in Alaska and Hawaii. Only one state, Vermont, has enacted a "civil union" gay marriage bill that permits same-sex couples to marry (recent strides in Canada, France, Sweden, Norway, Denmark, Iceland, Germany, and the Netherlands have resulted in the adoption of similar protections).[5]

Criminalization of Consensual Sexual Activity

Currently, eighteen states criminalize private consensual sexual activity between adults in a number of ways. Criminal offenses of this type may be generally worded to cover what is called "unnatural" sex acts or "crimes against nature," or they may single out "sodomy" (which is usually defined as including oral and anal sex) in particular. Currently five states (Arkansas, Kansas, Missouri, Oklahoma, and Texas) have laws that specifically criminalize only same-sex consensual sexual activity. The remaining thirteen states that criminalize consensual sexual activity (Alabama, Alaska, Arizona, Florida, Idaho, Louisiana, Massachusetts, Minnesota, Mississippi, North Carolina, South Carolina, Utah, and Virginia) do so for certain acts such as oral or anal intercourse—regardless of the sex of the parties. The penalties available for offenses such as these range from thirty days to life imprisonment.[6]

Hate Crimes

Twenty-three states and the District of Columbia have established some sort of mechanism to respond to and/or record information about hate crimes related to sexual orientation. Although the federal Hate Crimes Statistics Act requires the U.S. Justice Department to collect and report information about hate violence related to sexual orientation, recording and reporting of information by all local police agencies is not required. Consequently, information about hate violence motivated by sexual orientation and gender identity on a national scale is scarce.

Gays, lesbians, and bisexuals remain a class of people in our society that continues to face hatred and intolerance. The inability to live one's life freely—to be ridiculed, shunned, perpetually fearful and circumspect, or physically harmed for it—creates extraordinary pressures as well as emotional, pyschological, and physical strains that most people cannot even begin to feel or imagine. These incomparable factors certainly elevate the degree to which employers are challenged in their overall efforts to manage diversity in the workplace.

Strategies for Managing Diversity in Sexual Orientation

Clearly, the formidable challenges facing gays, lesbians, and bisexuals go well beyond the workplace. Although employers certainly cannot be expected to redress the homophobia that pervades our society, they can create a work environment that is safe and free of hatred and violence.

Eradicating Discrimination in the Workplace

Since 1974, the U.S. Congress has introduced bills, mirroring other civil rights laws, that would prohibit employment discrimination in the public and private sectors based on sexual orientation. By 1995, when the Employment Non-Discrimination Act (ENDA) was introduced, there were a record 138 sponsors. Each year, a new bill is introduced with more and more sponsors; however, each year the bills are defeated, despite the fact that there is increasing public support for such a law. Several recent polls, for example, consistently indicate that American adults support equal employment protection for persons of all sexual orientations:

   1995. A poll by *Newsweek* magazine taken among actual voters showed that 84 percent supported equal rights for gays and lesbians in the workplace.

   May 1996. A *Newsweek* poll showed that 84 percent of American adults supported equal protections in employment for gays and lesbians.

   June 1996. A poll by the Associated Press showed that 85 percent of adults favor federal legislation to give equal protection in employment to gays and lesbians.

   November 1996. Greenberg Research, Inc., conducted a national survey of 1,007 voters at election time. They found that:
   1. Among Christians generally, 70 percent believe that gays and lesbians should be protected from discrimination in the workplace; 23 percent do not.
   2. Among evangelical Christians, 60 percent are in favor while 34 percent are not.

   July 1998. A public opinion poll with a margin of error of 4 percent was conducted by the Princeton Survey Research Associates for *Newsweek* magazine on July 30–31, 1998. It found that 83 percent of the general population felt gays and lesbians deserve equal rights in obtaining jobs. Legislators will ignore these poll data at their peril.[7]

Public sentiment over employment protections for gays, lesbians, and bisexuals was perhaps galvanized by the "gays in the military" debacle. President Clinton was successful in getting the question of whether or not a person was a "homosexual" dropped from the military application form. It was dropped as part of a compromise between President Clinton and the U.S. Congress over the issue of officially allowing gays and lesbians to serve in the armed forces. However, the compromise resulted in the "Don't Ask, Don't Tell" policy, which effectively says the military will allow gays and lesbians in, but they'll be dismissed if they make their sexuality known.[8]

In his second term as president, however, Clinton, on May 28, 1998, issued Executive Order 13087, which reaffirmed the long-standing internal executive branch policy prohibiting discrimination based on sexual orientation within *civilian* employment. The executive order adds sexual orientation to the list of categories for which discrimination is prohibited (i.e., race, color, religion, gender, national origin, disability, and age). The policy states that a person's sexual orientation should not be the basis for the denial of a job or a promotion. This executive order represents the first time that the prohibition against sexual orientation discrimination has appeared in a specific directive from the president.

It should further be noted, however, that the Office of Personnel Management (OPM) has long interpreted federal law in such a manner that employment decisions will be made on the basis of a person's ability to perform his or her work, and not such factors as sexual orientation. Although the Civil Service Reform Act of 1978 does not explicitly prohibit discrimination on the basis of sexual orientation, one section of the act, 5 U.S.C. §2302(b)(10), prohibits federal employers from discriminating against employees on the basis of conduct that does not adversely affect employee performance. Thus OPM has interpreted this statute as prohibiting discrimination based on sexual orientation.[9]

Federal employees and applicants who perceive that they are being discriminated against based on sexual orientation can seek relief from the U.S. Merit Systems Protection Board (MSBP), the Office of Special Counsel, an independent agency within the executive branch, or through negotiated or agency grievance procedures. However, relief cannot be sought from the U.S. Equal Employment Opportunity Commission

(EEOC) or through a lawsuit, because, as noted, there are no federal laws that proscribe employment discrimination based on sexual orientation. Of course, gay, lesbian, or bisexual employees or applicants for a federal job may never choose to seek relief from alleged or perceived employment discrimination for fear that it would further stigmatize them or result in the risky move of "publicly" coming out of the closet.

As already noted, several states and localities have issued protections for gays, lesbians, and bisexuals in the workplace. At least nineteen states and over 144 cities and counties, including Washington, D.C., have statutes, executive orders, or ordinances prohibiting discrimination against public employees based on sexual orientation. Table 8.1 shows the breakdown of states that offer such protections.

As part of an overall diversity program, it is important that public employers without nondiscrimination policies work to promote formal protections for gays, lesbians, and bisexuals in their workforces. This is critical for creating an overall safe environment for all employees. Employers having such policies need to ensure that they are adequately enforced. Some studies question whether the statutes, executive orders, and ordinances are adequately enforced, and the extent to which gays, lesbians, and bisexuals are filing claims. As noted earlier, however, a decision to file a grievance is difficult, since it requires the individual to publicly come out of the closet, which is risky for many.[10] In addition, as other studies show, gays and lesbians perceive that they are unlikely to receive a fair shake in the court system, so they never come forward with complaints of discrimination.[11]

As Loden explains, it is essential that organizations create antidiscrimination policies to protect gays and lesbians in the workplace so as to guarantee "the right of every individual to inclusion, respect, cooperation, and equal treatment."[12]

Eradicating Harassment on the Job

Another form of discrimination on the job is harassing behavior because of sexual orientation. As noted in Chapter 5, in 1998 the U.S. Supreme Court widened workplace sexual harassment claims in *Oncale v. Sundowner Offshore Services*[13] when it ruled that same-sex sexual harassment in the workplace is actionable as sex discrimination under Title VII of the Civil Rights Act of 1964 as amended. In this unanimous decision, the *Oncale* Court ruled that it was the conduct itself, and not the sex or motivation of the people involved, that determined whether sexual

TABLE 8.1   States That Prohibit Discrimination Against Public and Private Sector Employees Based on Sexual Orientation

State	Type/Year Passed or Issued
California	Statute/1992 (includes private)
Colorado	Executive Order/1990
Connecticut	Statute/1991 (includes private)
Hawaii	Statute/1991 (includes private)
Iowa	Executive Order/1999
Maryland	Executive Order/1993
Massachusetts	Statute/1989 (includes private)
Minnesota	Statute/1993 (includes private)
Nevada	Statute/1999
New Hampshire	Statute/1998
New Jersey	Statute/1992 (includes private)
New Mexico	Executive Order/1985
New York	Executive Order/1983
Ohio	Executive Order/1988
Pennsylvania	Executive Order/1988
Rhode Island	Statute/1995 (includes private)
Vermont	Statute/1992 (includes private)
Washington	Executive Order/1993
Wisconsin	Statute/1982 (includes private)

Source: Adapted from Roddrick A. Colvin, "Improving State Policies Prohibiting Public Employment Discrimination Based on Sexual Orientation," *Review of Public Personnel Administration,* Spring 2000, pp. 5-19; and Wayne van der Meide, *Legislating Equality: A Review of Laws Affecting Gay, Lesbian, Bisexual, and Transgendered People in the United States* (Washington, D.C.: National Gay and Lesbian Task Force, 2000).

harassment amounted to discrimination because of sex. The Court said that sexual desire, whether homosexual or heterosexual, is not a necessary element of such a case under the Civil Rights Act of 1964 as amended. The Court concluded that a "plaintiff who brings a same-sex sexual harassment claim under Title VII must prove that the conduct at issue was not merely tinged with offensive sexual connotations, but actually constituted discrimination because of sex."[14]

Notwithstanding the Supreme Court's *Oncale* decision, lower courts continue to be divided as to whether same-sex harassment is covered under the Civil Rights Act as amended.[15] For example, in *Simonton v.*

Runyon,[16] the U.S. Court of Appeals for the Second Circuit dismissed a claim of harassment on the basis of sexual orientation on the grounds that Title VII of the Civil Rights Act as amended does not prohibit discrimination based on sexual orientation. The court interpreted the *Oncale* ruling in this fashion:

> *Oncale* did not suggest . . . that male harassment of other males always violates Title VII. *Oncale* emphasized that every victim of such harassment must show that he was harassed because he was male. . . . Subsequent to the Supreme Court's decision in *Oncale*, the First Circuit has reaffirmed the inapplicability of Title VII to discrimination based on sexual orientation. . . . We likewise do not see how *Oncale* changes our well-settled precedent that "sex" refers to membership in a class delineated by gender. The critical issue, as stated in *Oncale*, "is whether members of one sex are exposed to disadvantageous terms or conditions of employment to which members of the other sex are not exposed." Simonton has alleged that he was discriminated against not because he was a man, but because of his sexual orientation. Such a claim remains non-cognizable under Title VII.[17]

It would seem from *Simonton*, as well as other cases decided after the U.S. Supreme Court's *Oncale* ruling, that lower courts are willing to accept a Title VII cause of action claim on same-sex harassment cases if the plaintiff argues that he or she is being harassed because of sex, not because of sexual orientation.[18] Indeed, some courts are using this same standard set forth in *Oncale* in broader discrimination suits that involve the sexual identity of the plaintiff. In *Rosa v. Park West Bank & Trust Co.*,[19] for example, a man was denied the opportunity to apply for a bank loan because he was dressed as a woman. Lucas Rosa, the plaintiff, sued under the Equal Credit Opportunity Act (ECOA) on the grounds that the bank refused to provide him with a loan application because he was not dressed in "masculine attire" and the refusal amounted to sex discrimination under the ECOA.

The Court of Appeals for the First Circuit in *Rosa* ruled first that the district court was correct in saying that the prohibited bases of discrimination under the ECOA do not include style of dress or sexual orientation. But, the court noted, this is not the discrimination that the plaintiff alleges. Rather, the court goes on to say, Rosa is alleging that the bank's actions were taken, in whole or in part, on the basis of Rosa's sex. The court concludes, then, that the proper standard in determining whether or not Rosa was discriminated against rests on "sex-based discrimination" or "a theory of sex discrimination," and not discrimination based on manner of dress or perceived sexual orientation.[20]

An interesting development around harassment based on sexual orientation has developed around bisexuals. In *Holman v. Indiana*, the U.S. Court of Appeals for the Seventh Circuit, in a truly obfuscating decision, stated that

> Title VII does not cover the "equal opportunity" or "bisexual" harasser, because such a person is not discriminating on the basis of sex; [the] equal opportunity harasser is not treating one sex better or worse than the other, but is treating both sexes the same, albeit badly.[21]

It should be noted that in jurisdictions where statutes, executive orders, or ordinances explicitly proscribe discrimination on the basis of sexual orientation (see Table 8.1), state courts are finding that same-sex harassment is actionable under those specific provisions. For example, in *Murray v. Oceanside Unified School District*,[22] the Court of Appeal of California for the Fourth Appellate District found that alleged victims of harassment based on sexual orientation have a cause of action under California's state law prohibiting discrimination based on sexual orientation. The court found that the plaintiff "should be allowed the opportunity to seek to prove a pattern of continuing violations of the public policy against workplace harassment on the basis of sexual orientation."[23]

The point to be made from this cursory review of case law around same-sex harassment is that if employers are genuinely committed to creating a hostile-free work environment, they will incorporate in their existing sexual harassment policies and programs proscriptions against harassment based on sexual orientation. Ensuring that the policy is enforced will send the message to everyone in the workplace that discrimination or harassment based on sexual orientation will not be tolerated.

In addition, federal employers are challenged to enforce Executive Order 13087, and state and local governments the prevailing statutes, executive orders, or ordinances in their jurisdictions in a manner that protects *all* workers from sexual harassment. These measures will obviously prove significant for a healthy and productive workforce.

Developing Family Friendly Benefits and Policies

With benefits composing approximately 40 percent of a worker's compensation, employees who can obtain benefits for their spouses are, in effect, paid more than employees—heterosexual as well as gay—in relationships that are not legally recognized. The ability of employers to address this disparity will lead toward greater economic justice for everyone in the workplace.

Domestic Partner Benefits. Perhaps the most critical type of family-friendly policy that gays, lesbians, and bisexuals have pushed for in the past several years is domestic partner benefits. Although there is no universal definition of the term "domestic partner," it generally connotes, from an employment standpoint, two people living together and includes requirements relating to age, blood relationship, and emotional commitment. The major difference is that, unlike marriage, two persons of the same sex are allowed to be domestic partners.[24]

Some public and private sector employers across the country have begun to offer benefits such as health insurance, sick leave, and life insurance to the domestic partner of an employee. To date, only seven states and the District of Columbia offer some kind of domestic partner employment benefits to all or some of their state employees: California, Delaware, Hawaii, Massachusetts, New York, Oregon, and Vermont. At the local level, there are eighty-three municipal governments (i.e., cities and counties) that offer some employment benefits to the domestic partners of their employees.[25] Outside the United States, a small handful of countries and provinces, including Denmark, Norway, France, and the province of Ontario, Canada, also offer such benefits.

The issue of domestic partner benefits has generated a good deal of controversy, centered mainly around the notion that governments should not recognize a family relationship between lesbians, gay men, or heterosexual partners who are not legally married. Other critics maintain that even though the costs of domestic partner benefits are relatively low (see Table 8.2), they drive up the costs of overall employee benefit programs. Many have argued, however, that as we move into the next century and employers seek to recruit and retain quality employees, governments must recognize the right of employees to construct family relationships in the way they so desire.

One interesting new development as of this writing is sex-change benefit coverage for city employees in San Francisco. It is the only government body in the nation to make such benefits available. The state of Minnesota at one time offered such benefits, but they were invalidated in 1998. The benefit provides up to $50,000 to city workers who seek to

TABLE 8.2   Costs of Health Benefits for Domestic Partners

Public Employer	Year Enacted	Cost of D.P. Health Benefits as % of Total Health Costs
Seattle, Wash.	1990	1.1
San Francisco, Calif.	1991	-[a]
Berkeley, Calif.	1985	3.0
San Mateo County, Calif.	1992	0.7
Santa Cruz City, Calif.	1986	-[a]
Santa Cruz County, Calif.	1988	-[a]
West Hollywood, Calif.	1989	2.0
Laguna Beach, Calif.	1990	-[a]

Notes:

[a] Public employers reported that the additional cost was so negligible that no analysis has been done to determine the cost of coverage.

Source: Dennis Hostetler and Joan E. Pynes. "Domestic Partnership Benefits: Dispelling the Myth," *Review of Public Personnel Administration*, Winter 1995, p. 54.

change their gender. The cost of male-to-female surgery is about $37,000, and female-to-male surgery is $77,000. The benefit could also cover hormone therapy and other related procedures. Transgender advocates have praised the symbolic value of the benefits.[26]

Training to Combat Negative Stereotypes

As noted throughout this book, myths and negative stereotypes about people will greatly affect their attitudes and ultimately work behaviors. Tables 8.3 and 8.4 illustrate some of the common stereotypes and myths about gays, lesbians, and bisexuals. A particularly fatuous one, as it pertains to federal employment, is that gays and lesbians represent security risks. The belief is that gays or lesbians would be more susceptible to blackmail because of their sexual orientation and therefore should not be

TABLE 8.3   Commonly Held Sexual Orientation Stereotypes

Lesbians and gay men	Should not be parents; sexual beings first and foremost; sexually aggressive, hit on straights; unclean and unholy; choose not to be straight
Heterosexuals	Insensitive; homophobic; uptight about own sexuality; "less feminine" women are seen as dykes; "less masculine" men are seen as queers.

Source: Adapted from Marilyn Loden and Judy B. Rosener *Workforce America!* Homewood, Ill.: Business One Irwin (1991).

granted security clearances in the federal government. This has been a myth, however, because there have been no known cases of gay-related blackmail for espionage.[27]

It is axiomatic that government employers will need to develop training programs to combat the negative attitudes and stereotypes that managers and workers have toward gays, lesbians, and bisexuals. As noted previously, these negative attitudes serve as a major obstacle to successfully managing diverse workforces and can ultimately have a negative effect on productivity and work motivation. Just as most private and nonprofit organizations that provide diversity training now include a component addressing sexual orientation, in-house government training programs would be well served to do the same.

The U.S. Army, in January 2000, did just that. It ordered mandatory sensitivity training around gay issues and concerns for all soldiers. Unfortunately, it came in the aftermath of the murder of a soldier, Private Barry Winchell, at Fort Campbell, Kentucky. Winchell was killed in July 1999 by a barracks mate who believed him to be gay. Private Calvin N. Glover was court-martialed for the killing and sentenced to life in prison. The training order is part of the military's drive to rid the ranks of anti-gay actions and statements.

Although the military's training program came in reaction to a violent hate crime, many employers have been more proactive in launching programs to combat negative stereotypes around sexual orientation. One example is in Medley, Florida, where Police Chief Patrick M. Kelly promotes and endorses the need for diversity training. Kelly added sexual orientation to Medley Police Department's nondiscrimination policy after he became chief seven years ago. Kelly works with groups such as Florida LEGAL, a statewide group of about fifty gay and lesbian police

TABLE 8.4 Common Myths Associated with Gays, Lesbians, and Bisexuals

Myth 1	Gays cluster in certain occupations such as hair stylist, dancer, nurse or more "feminine" jobs.
Myth 2	People who associate with gays, lesbians, or bisexuals are probably gay, lesbian, or bisexual themselves.
Myth 3	Gays, lesbians, or bisexuals in sensitive or high-level jobs are security risks. The notion is that because they keep their sexual orientation secret, they are easier targets for blackmail. This rationale kept gays out of public employment, particularly in the 1950s McCarthy era.
Myth 4	Gays, lesbians, or bisexuals don't have normal, lasting relationships. This is because they are believed to be abnormal and promiscuous.
Myth 5	Gay men act feminine and lesbians act masculine.
Myth 6	Gays, lesbians, or bisexuals are a bad influence on children. The extreme form of this myth rests in the belief that gays, lesbians, or bisexuals are sexual perverts, and would therefore tend to be child molesters.

Source: Adapted from Norma Carr-Ruffino, *Diversity Success Strategies* (Boston: Butterworth Heinemann, 1999), pp. 211–212.

officers that assists law enforcement departments in their efforts to tear down the negative, prevailing perceptions of gay and lesbian uniformed officers. Kelly is also chair of the Florida Department of Law Enforcement's Criminal Justice Standards and Training Commission, which establishes and enforces police rules and policies. Not only is he well-versed on diversity issues, but he also runs a management consulting firm that specializes in police diversity training, which includes discrimination based on sexual orientation.[28]

One important point to be gleaned from the above example is that if police departments, which have tended to be one of the least progressive employers on gay issues, are making some progress in combating negative stereotypes against gays and lesbians, other government organizations should be challenged to follow suit.

Conclusion

An area of diversity management that is particularly challenging for government employers is sexual orientation. For one thing, the identity of gay, lesbian, and bisexual workers is masked or camouflaged. Although they have the option of making their identity known, it is only recently, as a result of raised social consciousness, that it has been somewhat safe for them to do so. Making the workplace safe for gays, lesbians, and bisexuals is also very critical because discrimination based on sexual orientation is still not covered in any federal law. As American society becomes increasingly diverse in every way, government employers have the opportunity to develop programs and policies that can ultimately improve their effectiveness in serving the needs and interests of the American people.

Notes

1. See Gregory Lewis and Howard Taylor, "Public Opinion Toward Gay and Lesbian Teachers," *Review of Public Personnel Administration* 21 (2001): 133–151.

2. Ibid.

3. Norma Carr-Ruffino, *Diversity Success Strategies* (Boston: Butterworth Heinemann, 1999).

4. *Boy Scouts of America v. James Dale*, 530 U.S. 640 (2000).

5. See, for example, "Same-Sex Dutch Couples Gain Marriage and Adoption Rights," *New York Times*, December 20, 2000, p. A8.

6. See Wayne van der Meide, *Legislating Equity: A Review of Laws Affecting Gay, Lesbian, Bisexual, and Transgendered People in the United States* (Washington, D.C.: National Gay and Lesbian Task Force, 2000).

7. See http://www.religioustolerance.org/hom_empl.htm.

8. Charles W. Gossett, "Lesbians and Gay Men in the Public Sector Workforce," in Carolyn Ban and Norma M. Riccucci, eds., *Public Personnel Management: Current Concerns, Future Challenges*, 3d ed. (New York: Longman, 2001).

9. See U.S. Office of Personnel Management (OPM), *Addressing Sexual Orientation Discrimination in Federal Civilian Employment: A Guide to Employees' Rights* (Washington, D.C., 1999).

10. See Norma M. Riccucci and Charles W. Gossett, "Employment Discrimination in State and Local Government: The Lesbian and Gay Male Experience," *American Review of Public Administration*, June 1996, pp. 175–200.

11. R. Rivera, "Queer Law: Sexual Orientation in the Mid-Eighties, Part 1," *University of Dayton Law Review* 10 (1985): 459–540.

12. Marilyn Loden, *Implementing Diversity* (Chicago: Irwin Professional Publishing, 1996), p. 85.

13. *Oncale v. Sundowner Offshore Services*, 523 U.S. 75 (1998).

14. *Oncale v. Sundowner Offshore Services* (1998) at p. 75.

15. See, for example, Gossett, "Lesbians and Gay Men"; and Ronald Turner, "The Unenvisaged Case, Interpretive Progression, and Justiciability of Title VII Same-Sex Sexual Harassment Claims," *Duke Journal of Gender Law and Policy* 7 (2000): 57; and Ramona Paetzold, "Same-Sex Sexual Harassment Revisited," *Employee Rights and Employment Policy Journal* 3 (1999): 251.

16. *Simonton v. Runyon*, 232 F.3d 33 (2d Cir. 2000).

17. *Simonton v. Runyon* (2000) at p. 36, citing *Oncale v. Sundowner Offshore Services* (1998) at p. 80.

18. See, for example, *Hamner v. St. Vincent Hospital and Health Care Center*, 224 F.3d 701 (7th Cir. 2000).

19. *Rosa v. Park West Bank & Trust Co.*, 214 F.3d 213 (1st Cir. 2000).

20. *Rosa v. Park West Bank & Trust Co.* (2000) at p. 215.

21. *Holman v. Indiana*, 211 F.3d 399 (7th Cir. 2000) at p. 399. It should be further noted, however, that discrimination against an employee because of bisexuality is not prohibited by Title VII of the Civil Rights Act as amended. See Gossett, "Lesbians and Gay Men."

22. *Murray v. Oceanside Unified School District*, 79 Cal. App. 4th 1338 (2000).

23. *Murray v. Oceanside Unified School District* (2000) at p. 1363.

24. See Charles W. Gossett, "Domestic Partnership Benefits," in Jay M. Shafritz, ed., *International Encyclopedia of Public Policy and Administration* (Boulder: Westview, 1998), pp. 706–707.

25. Van der Meide, *Legislating Equality*.

26. "Sex-Change Coverage to San Francisco Workers," *New York Times*, February 18, 2001, p. 20.

27. See, for example, Anthony Patrick Carnevale and Susan Carol Stone, *The American Mosaic* (New York: McGraw-Hill, 1995).

28. See Steve Rothaus, "Police Group Seeks to Dispel Stereotype About Gay Officers," *Miami Herald*, September 14, 2000; http://www.gaymilitary.ucsb.edu/news9_14_00b.htm.

Additional Reading

Brookins, Robert. "A Rose by Any Other Name . . . The Gender Basis of Same-Sex Sexual Harassment." *Drake Law Review* 46 (1998): 441–466.

Colker, Ruth. "A Bisexual Jurisprudence." *Law and Sexuality* 3 (1993): 127–137.

Colvin, Roddrick A. "Improving State Policies Prohibiting Public Employment Discrimination Based on Sexual Orientation." *Review of Public Personnel Administration*, Spring 2000, pp. 5–19.

Davila-Caballero, Jose. "Sexual Orientation and Same-Sex Harassment After *Oncale v. Sundowner*." *Revista Juridica de la Universidad de Puerto Rico* 69 (2000): 317–342.

DelPo, Marianne C. "The Thin Line Between Love and Hate: Same-Sex Hostile-Environment Sexual Harassment." *Santa Clara Law Review* 40 (1999): 1–26.

Donovan, James M. "An Ethical Argument to Restrict Domestic Partnerships to Same-Sex Couples." *Law and Sexuality* 8 (1998): 649–670.

Eisemann, Vanessa H. "Protecting the Kids in the Hall: Using Title IX to Stop Student-on-Student Anti-Gay Harassment." *Berkeley Women's Law Journal* 15 (2000): 125–160.

Gossett, Charles W. "Domestic Partnership Benefits." In Jay M. Shafritz, ed., *International Encyclopedia of Public Policy and Administration*, pp. 706–707. Boulder: Westview, 1998.

_____. "Domestic Partnership Benefits: Public Sector Patterns." *Review of Public Personnel Administration* 14 (1994): 64–84.

_____. "Lesbian and Gay Men in the Public Sector Workforce." In Carolyn Ban and Norma M. Riccucci, eds., *Public Personnel Management: Current Concerns, Future Challenges.* 3d ed. New York: Longman, 2001.

Haeberle, S. H. "Gay Men and Lesbians at City Hall." *Social Science Quarterly* 77 (1996): 190–197.

Harvard Law Review Association, ed. *Sexual Orientation and the Law.* Cambridge: Harvard University Press, 1989.

Horne, Philip S. "Challenging Public- and Private-Sector Schemes Which Discriminate Against Unmarried Opposite-Sex and Same-Sex Partners." *Law and Sexuality* 4 (1994): 35–52.

Hostetler, Dennis W., and Joan E. Pynes. "Domestic Partnership Benefits: Dispelling the Myth." *Review of Public Personnel Administration,* Winter 1995, pp. 41–59.

_____. "'Don't Ask, Don't Tell' Prevails in Boy Scouts." *Nonprofit Management and Leadership,* Winter 2000, pp. 235–237.

_____. "Sexual Orientation Discrimination and Its Challenges for Nonprofit Managers." *Nonprofit Management and Leadership,* Fall 2000, pp. 49–63.

Katz, Jonathon Ned. *Gay American History: Lesbians and Gay Men in the U.S.A.* Rev. ed. New York: Meridian, 1992.

Lehman, Brian. "The Equal Protection Problem in Sexual Harassment Doctrine." *Columbia Journal of Gender and Law* 10 (2000): 125–161.

Leonard, Arthur S. *Gay and Lesbian Rights Protections in the U.S.* Washington, D.C.: National Gay and Lesbian Task Force, 1989.

Lewis, Gregory B. "Lifting the Ban on Gays in the Civil Service: Federal Policy Towards Gay and Lesbian Employees Since the Cold War." *Public Administration Review* 57, no. 5 (1997): 387–395.

McFarland, Deborah N. "Beyond Sex Discrimination: A Proposal for Federal Sexual Harassment Legislation." *Fordham Law Review,* October 1996, pp. 493–542.

Riccucci, Norma M., and Charles W. Gossett. "Employment Discrimination in State and Local Government: The Lesbian and Gay Male Experience." *American Review of Public Administration,* June 1996, pp. 175–200.

Rienzo, Barbara A., James W. Button, and Kenneth D. Wald. "Conflicts over Sexual Orientation Issues in the Schools." In Elaine B. Sharp, ed., *Culture Wars and Local Politics.* Lawrence: University Press of Kansas, 1999.

Schultz, Vicki. "Reconceptualizing Sexual Harassment." *Yale Law Journal* 107 (1998): 1683–1706.

Smallets, Sonya. "Oncale v. Sundowner Offshore Services: A Victory for Gay and Lesbian Rights?" *Berkeley Women's Law Journal* 14 (1999): 136–148.

U.S. Office of Personnel Management. *Addressing Sexual Orientation Discrimination in Federal Civilian Employment: A Guide to Employees' Rights.* Washington, D.C., 1999.

Van der Meide, Wayne. 2000. *Legislating Equality: A Review of Laws Affecting Gay, Lesbian, Bisexual, and Transgendered People in the United States.* Washington, D.C.: National Gay and Lesbian Task Force.

Wald, K. D., J. W. Button, and B. A. Rienzo. "The Politics of Gay Rights in American Communities: Explaining Antidiscrimination Ordinances and Policies." *American Journal of Political Science* 40 (1996): 1152–1178.

Yamada, David C. "The Phenomenon of 'Workplace Bullying' and the Need for Status-Blind Hostile Work Environment Protection." *Georgetown Law Journal*, March 2000, pp. 475–536.

Yang, A. S. "Attitudes Toward Homosexuality." *Public Opinion Quarterly* 61 (1997): 477–507.

9

Epilogue:
Public Sector Organizations
Positioning for the Future

Traditionally and historically, people of European ancestry have tended to dominate public and private sector organizations, with men of European ancestry running them. This has changed and will continue to change during the twenty-first century. By 2020, women and men will each compose about half of the total workforce, and a growing percentage of the workforce will be made up of African Americans, Latinos, and Asian Americans.[1]

Public sector organizations have recognized that a diverse workplace is a critical ingredient for continued success. As government workforces become increasingly diverse, public employers are poised to improve the way in which government operates and is perceived by the general citizenry. Taking explicit steps to create an atmosphere in which all workers feel welcomed, valued, and essential enhances employee satisfaction and productivity. Effectively managing diversity is not only sound human resources practice, but it makes good "business" sense. That is, it enables government agencies to ultimately position themselves to improve their public image and their ability to effectively govern.

Successfully managing diversity is a challenging process, but with a clear vision, careful planning, strong leadership, and a willingness and commitment to change, government can develop a competitive advantage as an employer and a producer of services to the American people.

In addition to organizational-level reforms, however, the government has the further responsibility of working to alleviate one of the most pernicious obstacles to successfully managed and run diversity programs—

disparities in the educational system. The ability to ensure a quality education for *everyone* is perhaps the sine qua non to a quality workforce. *Workforce 2020,* for example, points out that the jobs of the twenty-first century will be substantially different from those in existence today. A number of jobs in the least-skilled job classes will shrink, while high-skilled professions will grow rapidly. The report goes on to say that education is key for the jobs of tomorrow:

> Upward mobility in the labor force depends, quite simply, on education. The single most important goal of workforce development must be to improve the quality of American public education substantially.[2]

Workforce 2020 further points out that the future of people of color is at greater risk because they are inadequately educated. Disparities in educational opportunities result in lower graduation rates for people of color compared with whites, and ultimately fewer and poorer job opportunities for them. The report strongly suggests that "tomorrow's minority workers can improve their position only if today's minority students are better educated."[3]

In short, if there is a serious commitment to providing African Americans, Latinos, and other protected classes with the broad-based skills and tools necessary, in the long run, to compete equally with whites for economic resources of any type in our society, they must be provided with a strong educational footing. This is obviously a critical prerequisite to the ability of *any* employer to develop effective diversity programs.

Notes

1. *Workforce 2020* (Indianapolis: Hudson Institute, 1997).
2. Ibid., pp. 8–9.
3. Ibid., p. 115.

INDEX

ADA (Americans with Disabilities
  Act), 5–6, 13–14, 123–124
  and the Eleventh Amendment, 131
  frequently asked questions about,
    128–129
  inclusion of learning disabilities in,
    133
  lawsuits associated with, 129–130
  and the use of health benefits, 134
Adarand v. Peña, 16
ADEA (Age Discrimination in
  Employment Act), 12, 14, 107–111
Adoption, 81
Advancing Women (report), 63
Advisory Commission on
  Intergovernmental Relations, 104
Advisory Council on Historic
  Preservation, 104
Advocate magazine, 139–140
Affirmative action: backlash against,
    48–49
  comparison of, with EEO and
    managing diversity, 2–3
  evolution of diversity from, 8
  evolution of, 11–22
  and glass ceilings, 71
  policy and law,
    importance of adhering to, 51–52
AFL-CIO, 95
African Americans: commonly-held
    stereotypes surrounding, 53–54
  increasing promotion opportunities
    for, 46–48
  and public employment, 37–46

and state/local government
  employment, 39
women, double disadvantage faced
  by, 71
African Development Council, 104
Age: as a bona fide occupational
    qualification (BFOQ), 110–111
  as a dimension of diversity, 28–30
  discrimination, eradicating, 107–111
  distribution of the labor force by, 7
  fact versus fiction regarding, 114
  federal civilian employment
    distribution by, 105–106
  reasonable factors other than
    (RFOA), 111
  sterotypes about, 112–113. *See also*
    Multigenerational workplaces
Agricultural and Transportation
    Barriers Compliance Board, 104
Agriculture, 86, 103–105, 133
Agriculture, Department of, 44, 69,
    103, 105, 124
AIDS (Acquired Immunodeficiency
    Syndrome), 14, 127, 130, 133
Air Force (United States), 103, 105
Alabama, 15, 141
Alabama Public Safety Department, 15
Alaska, 37–46, 140, 141
Alaska Natives, 37–46
Alternative work schedules, 85–89. *See
    also* Flextime
Amendments: Eleventh Amendment,
    110, 131
  Fifth Amendment, 15, 16, 19

155